5 21

The Endangered Sex

The
Endangered Sex

Neglect of Female Children in Rural North India

Barbara D. Miller

Cornell University Press, Ithaca and London

First published 1981 by Cornell University Press.
Published in the United Kingdom by Cornell University Press Ltd.,
Ely House, 37 Dover Street, London W1X 4HQ.

International Standard Book Number 0-8014-1371-0
Library of Congress Catalog Card Number 81-3226
Printed in the United States of America
*Librarians: Library of Congress cataloging information appears
on the last page of the book.*

To my parents

Contents

Tables

Figures

Preface

This is a book about children, some of whom are wanted and some of whom are not. It is also about the power of culture to shape family attitudes toward children and to determine how children are treated differently depending upon their sex. It is about India, but could have been written for many other parts of the world, too. In this book I discuss beliefs and practices that have very sad implications, that are depressing to research and describe, but that cannot be ignored if change is ever to occur.

It has often been noted that in Indian thought the processes of creation and destruction are inseparable, that one is the necessary counterpart of the other, indeed, that creation can come only from destruction. Fertility and mortality, growth and decay, female and male are likewise conjoined in a dramatic dynamic that unfolds in this book. For this is a story of how the birth of some inexorably brings the death of others, of how the survival of males feeds on the demise of females, of how the intense desire for sons is directly tied to the fatal neglect of daughters. The light and dark of Indian culture, the giving and taking, the benign and malign are simultaneously expressed in a twisted, tortured dance whose tempo continually increases.

The preponderance of males over females in the population of India has been a subject of concern and controversy since the late eighteenth century, when the practice of outright female infanticide in India was discovered by the British. This book addresses the fact of, and the reasons for, unbalanced sex ratios among children in present-day rural India and considers some of the cultural links between the present and the past.

Tackling the problem of sex ratio imbalances involves a complex web of related tasks. My first step is to examine sex ratios throughout the world and to explore how culture affects these ratios, especially among juveniles. I then sharpen my focus to India of the nineteenth century in order to demonstrate how the practice of outright female infanticide altered the proportions of the sexes at that time. A regional and social pattern of infanticide is uncovered: infanticide was most practiced in the Northwest and among the higher castes there. Next, sex ratio imbalances in twentieth-century India are presented with special consideration of sex ratios for the population under ten years of age. Here, too, we find a regional and social pattern, indeed, one very similar to that discovered for the practice of outright female infanticide during the nineteenth century. This correlation indicates a link between the earlier practice, which was outlawed and repressed by the government, and the current one of neglect and discrimination.

Later chapters inquire into the question of how, in an immediate sense, the proportions of the sexes among juveniles in rural India become unbalanced. I examine three factors: the allocation of food, of medical care, and of love. It is my proposition that an important part of the explanation for the discrimination against girls found in the North lies in the culturally mandated low demand for, and participation of, females in agricultural production there. I do recognize, however, that such an objective explanation does not account for the subjective feelings of most Indian peasants toward sons and daughters. The last sections of my book, therefore, explore the cultural foundations for strong son preference and daughter disfavor in the northern upper social strata. I have examined the roles of sons versus daughters in the North and South in terms of the need for heirs, for economic support in the parents' old age, ritual needs, and marriage costs. It is evident that daughters are much more a liability to parents in the North than in the South.

This book illustrates the powerful relationship between culture and mortality. Culture often plays an important role in determining those targeted for death; in this case the target group is North Indian girls, especially those of the higher social strata. The analysis also contributes to the study of women by exposing the strong effects of culture not only on female roles and status but also on female survival itself. Finally, those interested in development policy, particularly as it concerns population planning, will find relevant material in this book. Discrimination against girls is shown to act in tandem with preference for sons, so that more boys than girls survive than would otherwise be the case; these can be interpreted as indigenous mechanisms of "family planning" firmly embedded in the cultural matrix. Planners must take such mechanisms into account when they propose changes in fertility and mortality patterns, if change is to occur at all.

Female children in North India are indeed in great danger. Their chance of survival, compared with that of their brothers, is dramatically less. I argue that this survival differential stems primarily from cultural rather than natural causes. It is a "culture against females" in North India which brings into play the neglect and mistreatment of unknown numbers of children. Within this picture of gloom, however, one element of hope shines through. If culture rather than nature is to blame, then change is feasible, is more readily possible. Culture with its powerful rules and regulations does play havoc with human life, not just in India but everywhere in the world, for culture draws the targets of people who are to receive special care and those who are less worthy. But culture, once understood, is humanly mutable.

This book is aimed toward a greater understanding and thus perhaps an eventual conquering of the mortal caprices of one culture. It is a plea for the devotion of more research time and resources to the cultural causes of suffering and death and not just to their biological causes. It demands that scientists carefully consider the implications of the development of a sex-selective method of birth control which could very well result in a further scarcity of females and not only in North India. It is a painful reminder to those who think that aspects of modern technology bring blessings without costs and a dark question as to why those costs are most often borne by the female.

Throughout the past years many individuals and organizations have contributed to my work in major ways. A Woodrow Wilson Doctoral Dissertation Fellowship in Women's Studies enabled me to purchase microfilm copies of many unpublished dissertations and to travel to the libraries of Cornell University, the University of Wisconsin at Madison, and the University of Chicago. At the University of Chicago, the South Asia Reference Center, under the leadership of Maureen Patterson, was especially helpful in guiding me to several unpublished sources in its possession. A language fellowship from the American Institute of Indian Studies provided for a nine-month stay in India, where, in my spare time after Hindi classes, I was able to use libraries in Agra and Delhi and to meet several scholars who gave me much helpful advice and encouragement. A grant from the Rockefeller-Ford Research Program on Population and Development Policy made the completion of the research and the writing of this book possible, and I appreciate their generous support. Mary Kritz of the Rockefeller Foundation was a source of helpful advice during my grant tenure.

The Anthropology Department at Syracuse University, under the chairmanship of Glynn Cochrane, provided office space and typing assistance. Susan Wadley adeptly guided me through my graduate work. Michael Freedman was a constant source of wisdom, energy, and encouragement. David Sopher has been involved in a central way since the day he showed me a map of sex ratios in India which initiated the study. Fresh perspectives and helpful criticism from Glynn Cochrane were important contributions, as were the suggestions periodically offered by Agehananda Bharati. Moni Nag's demographic insights provided a challenge to me, one which I hope has been met. Barton Schwartz spurred me on with needling criticism and laconic humor.

Another extremely important group of people took the time, often a great deal of time, to answer a lengthy and tedious questionnaire. My feeling of gratitude to the scholars who responded to it—even if just to drop a note saying that they were unable to answer so many questions at that time—is immense. Those who completed the questionnaire in full are: P. C. Aggarwal, Christopher Fuller, Murray Leaf, John F. Marshall, Michael Moffatt, William H. Newell, Russell M. Reid, and Susan S. Wadley and Bruce W. Derr.

During the past several years many others in both India and the

United States have helped me in diverse ways—by discussing my work with me, sending articles, providing unpublished data, and giving encouragement. They include Shadbano Ahmed, R. A. Feldman, Gerry Forbes, Ruth Gabriel, Paul Greenough, David Gwatkin, Doranne Jacobson, Tom Kessinger, Betsey Lozoff, Joan Mencher, M. S. A. Rao, Thomas Ridgeway, A. R. Saiyed, Andrea Menefee Singh, and P. S. S. Sundar Rao.

The Cartographic Laboratory at Syracuse University, under the direction of D. Michael Kirchoff, is also thanked heartily, especially Eric Lindstrom, who created beautiful maps and charts out of the messy pieces of paper I took to him and whose enthusiasm for the project is appreciated. David Robinson of the Department of Geography gave helpful hints on the fine art of map making, particularly regarding the importance of scale. To help defray the costs of the cartographic work, the Maxwell School and the Office for Research and Graduate Affairs of Syracuse University provided a much appreciated grant.

Fellow students and workers at the Anthropology Department of Syracuse University helped in every way—collating questionnaires, typing, and raising my spirits. They are Susan Birns, Madge Cohen, Gail Fuller, Jeff Martin, Carol Pepe, Blake Thurman, Sharyn Weaver, and Ruth Willis. My current academic "home" at Syracuse's Local Revenue Administration Project is a bright spot in my life— made that way by my "chief," Glynn Cochrane, and all the other members of the LRAP team, especially Dayle Burnett, Charles de Burlo, Annette Earl, Alem Hailu, Rob Kent, Ruth Mara, and David Robinson. Jane Frost did a superb job of typing the final draft and deserves special mention. Barbara Burnham and Carol Betsch of Cornell University Press were pivotal in the final stages of preparing this work for publication.

For permission to use the base maps of India and Uttar Pradesh, I am grateful to Cornell University Press. They are reprinted from David E. Sopher, ed., *An Exploration of India,* copyright © 1980 by Cornell University. Parts of Chapter 7 have been previously published as a paper, "Female Neglect and the Costs of Marriage in Rural India," in *Contributions to Indian Sociology,* July 1980, and sections of Chapter 5 are forthcoming as "Female Labor Participation and Female Seclusion in Rural India: A Regional Analysis," in *Economic Development and Cultural Change*.

As this work has moved along its various stages to published book, David Sopher has been a source of enthusiasm, wisdom, and wit. I am grateful for his continuing help.

BARBARA D. MILLER

Syracuse, New York

A Note on Indian Names
and Technical Terms

I have followed common English practice in the rendering of Indian words, phrases, and place names. If such words and phrases have become so naturalized into the English language as to appear in the *Random House Dictionary of the English Language* (unabridged edition, 1969), then the dictionary spelling is used. Otherwise the word or phrase is presented in italics with diacritics the first time it appears, thereafter in Roman without diacritics. Transliteration follows the style sheet published in the *Journal of Asian Studies* 22 (1963).

Place names that are common in English usage are rendered in their familiar form, thus Ganges not Ganga. Names of Indian districts are those in use at the time of the 1961 Census of India, since that census is the one I rely upon most heavily. Therefore I use Kaira instead of Kheda, and Poona instead of Pune. When discussing census material from 1961 I use the state names of Mysore and Madras instead of the current names Karnataka and Tamil Nadu; these latter, however, are now so common that I often use them instead of the earlier ones when discussing village studies done in the last decade. I do not provide diacritics with place names, therefore Konku and not Koṅku.

Caste names are not rendered with diacritics either, therefore the Udaiyar and not the UDaiyaar. To denote the plural form of a caste, I follow the rule that northern castes form their plurals by having "s" added at the end, therefore Jat becomes Jats. Southern castes are more problematic. The Tamil plural ending, for instance, is "ar," thus Udaiyar is a plural form and it would be redundant to add an "s." Most southern castes, then, are rendered in their plural form as given most commonly in the literature, that is, without an "s." There is one major exception. The term Paraiyan is now so familiar to Western ears that its plural is given as Paraiyans, and not the Tamil Paraiyar which is seen in print less often.

The Endangered Sex

1
Life and Death, Males and Females

We are faced with the fact of a scarcity of females in the northwestern plains of India, especially in the upper social stratum there. This scarcity can be seen in the proportions of the sexes among children in rural India which vary in a stark regional pattern: boys are numerically preponderant in the northern plains but nowhere else. Other kinds of data point to a greater preponderance of males in the upper social echelon in the North. These patterns demand an exploration: why are there more boys in northern upper-class groups and not elsewhere?

A strong beginning has been made in the delineation of regional cultures in India which can be followed here. Sopher proposes a North-South dichotomy in which "North" is geographically the northwestern plains area of India, and "South" is geographically the southeastern and far southern regions. Thus West Bengal in the east does not really fit in—it is neither North nor South—and the same applies to the Himalayan region (Sopher 1980:294–296). Sopher's North-South dichotomy is constructed of historical-cultural regions, regions that are very apt for this study.

The problem is even more interesting when the regions above are put into wider perspective in terms of both sex ratio patterns and women's roles and statuses.[1] Looking toward the Middle East from

1. Sex ratio refers to the number of males per hundred females or, occasionally, the number of males per thousand females. The reader's attention will be drawn to the changes in referent.

India, we see a region characterized by masculine sex ratios (El-Badry 1969) and oppressed women, though the variation in the latter is great. In contrast, if attention is turned from India toward Southeast Asia, the picture is the opposite: balanced sex ratios and greater sex egalitarianism. Though these are incautious generalizations, and more research is needed on all the areas mentioned, there does appear to be some justification for viewing the Vindhya-Narmada divide in India as a "great divide" between the "masculinism" of the Middle East through to Northwest India, and the "feminism" of South India to Southeast Asia. Exactly why the watershed of sexual status and survival is located where it is needs to be explored: this book is one step in that direction.

My goal is to explain how and why there are fewer females than males in North India and then to show how that situation might be changed. My perspective is one of holistic anthropology, with a dash of geography added, applied to a demographic problem rooted in a cultural matrix. In order to sort out the complex web of issues, I have organized the most important of them as follows. The second chapter developed as I read "around" the subject of sex ratio imbalances in order to get some perspective in which to place the evidence of female scarcity. This chapter draws on examples that demonstrate the interaction between culture and differential mortality patterns for age and sex groups, a fascinating area of cultural demography which has been relatively neglected. Next, I back away from the central problem in another direction—that of history. Using secondary reports from the British period in India, I draw a picture of where and by whom female infanticide was practiced in pre-twentieth-century India. Chapter 4 presents the regional and social variations in the juvenile sex ratios of rural India. (In the text, "juvenile" refers primarily to the population under ten years of age, though sometimes to other age groupings that will also be noted. In the fifth chapter I ask how sex ratios become imbalanced in rural North India—what are the direct causes of death? I examine three factors that could result in differential mortality rates between boys and girls: nutrition, medical care, and love.

In the following chapter, the sixth, I penetrate more dense territory as the question "why" is addressed. In this instance there seem to be at least two dimensions to the question. First, why do North Indian peasants *say* that girls are less desirable than boys and thus not quite so worthy of solicitude in terms of nutrition and health care? Second, what is the anthropologist's explanation? This juxtaposition of perspectives corresponds to the classic emic-etic distinction first delineated by the linguist Pike (1967) and later used by anthropologists, most notably Harris (1974) in his analysis of sacred cows, forbidden pigs, and other long-standing cultural puzzles. Regarding the emic-etic distinction, it is important to remember that insider's view and outsider's view are rarely mutually exclusive; there is often, on the contrary, considerable overlap. Their difference is simply one of perspective. In Chapter 6, I examine the etic interpretation of why girls are less favored than boys. My hypothesis is that "worth" is to a large extent related to work. In North Indian propertied groups females are largely excluded from agricultural work and thus less economically valuable. Chapter 7 brings us to the "emic" part of the explanation, or at least to a major portion of that explanation which is itself a complexly woven design. I here concentrate on marriage costs and their influence on family feeling about daughters as being either liabilities or blessings to family welfare.

In the eighth chapter I examine what appears in many ways to be a mirror image of the above. Instead of looking at discrimination against daughters, I examine preference for sons. This continues the emic analysis of the previous chapter for, in reality, what Indians perceive is a strong preference for sons rather than a clear dislike for daughters. The problem is that son preference is so strong in some areas of India and among some classes that daughters must almost logically suffer in order that families' perceived and culturally mandated needs are fulfilled.

My conception of the interplay between the forces of production, property, and population is central to the problem with which this book deals. As yet, in either anthropology or demography, there is no systematic theory uniting these forces and explaining the nature of the relationships between them. At this stage, I can hope only to begin building such a synthetic theory.

That the mode of production can influence population dynamics has been recognized at least since the time of Malthus and Marx. While I am not oriented theoretically toward classical Marxism, I do lean on some of its broad ideas. One of these is relevant to the understanding of the interplay between production and population. In contradiction to Malthus's attempt to define a universal law of population, Marx writes that distinct modes of production carry with them distinct population laws: ". . . every specific historic mode of production has its own special laws of population, historically valid within its limits alone. An abstract law of population exists for plants and animals only, and insofar as man has not interfered with them" (Meek 1971:23). Here Marx is referring to the relationship between the mode of production and the *size* of the population, the predominant concern of Malthus and his supporters. In order to render Marx's idea more meaningful for the building of a broader theory, an important addition must be made to it: besides influencing the size of the population, the mode of production may result in a characteristic age structure and sexual composition within the population. My work deals with the latter: the sexual profile of a population. The delineation of such a profile is an important step forward; the question why female survival varies between different modes of production may be answered only after such basic groundwork has been laid.

The ways in which property is manipulated within a society also have important effects on many demographic phenomena: population size, rate of population growth, population mobility, and sex ratio. This book is most concerned with the last of these—sex ratio. My hypothesis is that a mode of production in which females play an important part tends to be found in tandem with a system of inheritance granting females access to the major means of production which in rural India is usually land. On the other hand, a mode of production which excludes females from important productive roles will coexist with inheritance rules that also exclude females from access to the major means of production.

I do not view production (and the sexual division of labor associated with a particular mode of production) as a *determinant* of a particular system of inheritance. The relationship can best be understood by translating them into Pike's emic-etic terminology. In this way the mode of production corresponds to the etic perspective of the outside analyst; dispersal of property corresponds to the emic per-spective of the insider. Only by arranging production and property in this idealized fashion as two different, though tandem, perspectives, can their effects on population be demonstrated. Both production and property are determinants of population dynamics, perhaps with dif-fering weights in different cultures, but both must always be consid-ered. To ignore one or the other results in only a partial understand-ing of the demographic situation. (This is not to say that demographic processes and events never have an effect on production and proper-ty. To the contrary, such processes are significant; they are simply not my concern here.)

The important part that culture plays in affecting male and female roles in production and the control of property cannot be overempha-sized. It is culture that dictates the greater worth of males as both producers and heirs in much of India, and it is culture that ignores and undervalues the vital, though often invisible, roles that women play. In order that my model of the interaction between the forces of production, property, and population dynamics in rural India be more easily grasped, it has been represented in schematic form (Fig. 1). The figure should be read from bottom to top, a process that starts with what I perceive to be the most basic factor motivating the entire system: the nature of agricultural production and its demand for female labor. The reader then proceeds upward to the level of the exclusion or inclusion of females from production and property, then to the cultural valuation of children based upon sex, and finally, to the resultant sex ratios. The figure is divided vertically into two columns, the "North" and the "South."[2] Beyond their regional reference, these terms also have a social dimension such that what is "northern" applies mainly to the propertied groups of the North just as the "southern" model fits most accurately the propertied groups in the South.[3] Unpropertied groups in both the North and South have a characteristic sex ratio pattern more like one another's than like the propertied groups of their respective regions.

2. Henceforth the designation of these model regions will not be enclosed by quotation marks, but merely capitalized.
3. The classification of "propertied" and "unpropertied" groups is explained in Chapter 4.

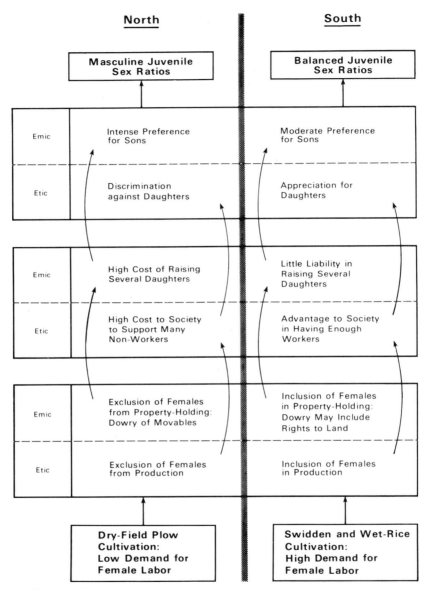

	North		South
	Masculine Juvenile Sex Ratios		**Balanced Juvenile Sex Ratios**
Emic	Intense Preference for Sons		Moderate Preference for Sons
Etic	Discrimination against Daughters		Appreciation for Daughters
Emic	High Cost of Raising Several Daughters		Little Liability in Raising Several Daughters
Etic	High Cost to Society to Support Many Non-Workers		Advantage to Society in Having Enough Workers
Emic	Exclusion of Females from Property-Holding: Dowry of Movables		Inclusion of Females in Property-Holding: Dowry May Include Rights to Land
Etic	Exclusion of Females from Production		Inclusion of Females in Production
	Dry-Field Plow Cultivation: Low Demand for Female Labor		**Swidden and Wet-Rice Cultivation: High Demand for Female Labor**

Figure 1 Production, property, and population in India: a North–South model

28

In general the northern model is characterized by higher rates of survival for juvenile males than females, the southern model by similar rates of survival for children of both sexes. The North tends to exclude females from both property and production; the South is more inclusive. While such a model as this has the obvious disadvantage of overidealizing the great amount of variety within these two dimensions of North and South, it also has advantages. First, precisely because the model idealizes, it allows us to discern more clearly the nature of divergences from it. This is important because some major divergences do exist. Second, it helps us to "sort out," even if somewhat artificially, the complex process by which both production and property influence one aspect of population dynamics in rural India.

The method of my inquiry is an unorthodox one for a cultural anthropologist. Generally one would perform field work and then undertake analysis on the basis of that field work. But the nature of the problem of sexual imbalances demands an all-India perspective in which regions and groups with notable imbalances in the proportions of the sexes are contrasted by controlled comparison with those without. Field work for one or two years in one or two villages would not provide an adequately broad basis for explanation of the problem.

I opted for a different approach: library research. The relatively wide ethnographic corpus on rural India and the voluminous collection of Indian censuses from the past one hundred years are my data base. This approach is based on my belief that ethnographies should be used, not just read, and that census data and ethnographies together can be merged to provide a broad yet detailed picture of Indian rural life.

In its basic form this inquiry follows the pattern established by Kolenda (1968, 1971) in her regional studies of family types in India and also by Tambiah (1973) in his examination of variations in marriage payments in South and Southeast Asia; both authors gathered and analyzed evidence from village studies. But their method possesses some faults which I hope to correct. The major problem stems from the small number of studies employed.[4] This fault is related to

4. Though Kolenda uses many more studies in her 1968 paper than in her 1971 article.

the erroneous assumption that any *one* village is a sufficient base
from which to make generalizations about vast geographical regions,
an assumption made in spite of the fact that most anthropologists
would never claim that the villages they studied are "typical." I
reduce the dangers of such poor sampling by limiting the regions
examined and increasing the number of reports used for these regions. The areas upon which I concentrate are North India, with
emphasis on Punjab and western Uttar Pradesh, and the far South. I
do include studies done on villages in other regions of India in order
to provide a fuller picture.

There are problems involved in gathering a large body of ethnographic data for each of the two regions and for upper and lower social
categories. The best documented area is the North, the most fully
studied social category is the landed class. Studies of low castes and
classes are rare. Ethnographic studies done in the two southern states
of Madras (Tamil Nadu) and Andhra Pradesh are scarce while, in
contrast, those conducted in the southern state of Mysore (Karnataka)
abound. (It is highly possible that Mysore's wonderful climate, rather
than any pressing anthropological problems specific to that region,
has attracted the many researchers.) The topics most neglected in the
literature are the treatment of female children within the home and the
domestic status of females of all ages. To help amend this situation I
sent a lengthy questionnaire to over forty anthropologists who had
worked in Indian villages; about one-third of them responded in some
form or another. The sites and sources of research are presented here
in Figure 2 and Table 1.

From time to time I have augmented the use of published and
unpublished ethnographies and data from the questionnaires with
Census of India Village Survey Monographs. These monographs
cover a standard list of ethnographic topics and have been written for
at least a dozen villages in every state of India. While not intended as
a study of a "representative" village, the information if used carefully
provides a way of filling in remaining lacunae.[5]

For data on sex ratios and the rate of female participation in agricultural labor, my major sources are censuses of India. Census data
give a broad backdrop upon which the cultural details provided by

5. An example of a study that rather carelessly assumes the representativeness of
Village Survey Monographs is Adelman and Dalton (1971).

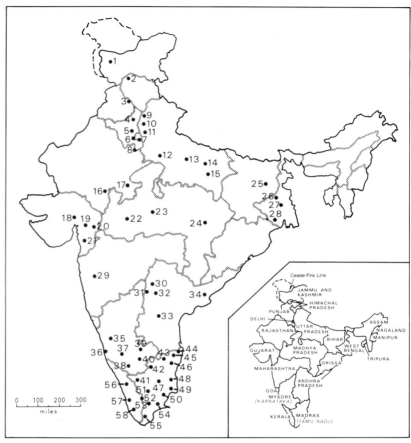

Figure 2 Sites and sources of ethnographic research. Numbers correspond to those in Table 1.

anthropologists can be sketched to advantage. In addition, I have gleaned information from dozens of disparate sources, such as historical studies and hospital reports, to help in the reconstruction and exploration of the system of female neglect and discrimination in North India.

There are several ways in which the findings of this work can function; the most important are as a study of the interaction of culture and population, as an analysis of regional and social varia-

Table 1
Sites and sources of ethnographic research

Index no.[a]	Village, district (state)	Sources
1	Utrassu-Umanagri, Anantnag (J. & K.)	Madan 1965
2	Goshen, Chamba (H.P.)	Newell 1952, 1965, 1978
3	Shahidpur, Ropar (Pun.)	Leaf 1972, 1978
4	Dhara, Karnal (Har.)	Morrison 1965
5	Badipur, Rohtak (Har.)	Miller 1975
6	Rampur (Del. Ter.)	Lewis 1965; Das Gupta 1977
7	Shanti Nagar (Del. Ter.)	Freed 1971; Freed and Freed 1971, 1973, 1976
8	Chavandi Kalan, Mewat area (Raj.-Har.-U.P.)	Aggarwal 1971, 1978
9	Khalapur, Saharanpur (U.P.)	Hitchcock 1956; Minturn 1976; Minturn and Hitchcock 1966
10	Shoron, Muzaffarnagar (U.P.)	Pradhan 1966
11	Bunkipur, Meerut (U.P.)	Marshall 1972, 1978
12	Karimpur, Mainpuri (U.P.)	Wadley 1975; Wadley and Derr 1978; Wiser 1936, 1978; Wiser and Wiser 1971
13	Mohana, Lucknow (U.P.)	Majumdar 1958
14	Sherupur, Faizabad (U.P.)	Gould 1959
15	Senapur and Madhopur (hamlet of Senapur), Jaunpur (U.P.)	Cohn 1954, 1972; Luschinsky 1962; Planalp 1956, 1971
16	Ranawaton-ki-Sadri, Chittorgarh (Raj.)	Chauhan 1967
17	Awan, Kota (Raj.)	Gupta 1974
18	Charotar villages, Kaira (Guj.)	Pocock 1972
19	Samiala, Baroda (Guj.)	Fukutake et al. 1964
20	Rajpur, Baroda (Guj.)	Maharaja Sayajirao University of Baroda 1970; Poffenberger 1975
21	Nokrigram and Saragram, Surat (Guj.)	Veen 1972
22	Ramkheri, Dewas (M.P.)	Mayer 1970
23	Nimkhera, Raisen (M.P.)	Jacobson 1970, 1972
24	Sasaholi, Bilaspur (M.P.)	Babb 1969
25	Bharko, Bagalpur (Bih.)	Shukla 1976
26	Supar, Birbhum (W. Ben.)	Fukutake et al. 1974
27	Kanchanpur, Burdwan (W. Ben.)	Basu 1962
28	Torkotala, Midnapore (W. Ben.)	Davis 1975
29	Gaon, Poona (Mah.)	Orenstein 1965
30	Fifteen villages, Medak (A.P.)	Singh 1969
31	Gopalpur, Hyderabad (A.P.)	Beals 1974
32	Shamirpet, Hyderabad (A.P.)	Dube 1967
33	Konduru, Kurnool (A.P.)	Hiebert 1971
34	Six villages, East Godavari (A.P.)	Reid 1971, 1978
35	Totagadde, Shimoga (Mys.)	Harper 1958, 1968; Wiltse Harper 1971
36	Three villages, South Kanara (Mys.)	Claus 1970
37	Chinnapura, Hassan (Mys.)	Regelson 1972
38	Rampura, Mysore (Mys.)	Srinivas 1976
39	Namhalli, Bangalore (Mys.)	Beals 1974

Table 1—*continued*

Index no.[a]	Village, district (state)	Sources
40	Elephant, Mysore (Mys.)	Beals 1974
41	Olappalaiyam, Coimbatore (Mad.)	Beck 1972
42	Nadupatti, Salem (Mad.)	Burkhart 1969, 1975
43	Reddiur, North Arcot (Mad.)	Montgomery 1972
44	MM, Chingleput (Mad.)	Mencher 1970
45	Thaiyur, Chingleput (Mad.)	Djurfeldt and Lindberg 1975, 1976
46	Endavur, Chingleput (Mad.)	Moffatt 1978, 1979
47	Parangudi, Tiruchirapalli (Mad.)	Moffatt 1978, 1979
48	Sripuram, Thanjavur (Mad.)	Béteille 1962, 1968
49	Thyagasamuthiram, Thanjavur (Mad.)	Sivertsen 1963
50	Kumbapettai, Thanjavur (Mad.)	Gough 1956
51	Tengalapatti, Madurai (Mad.)	Dumont 1957a, 1957b
52	Village near Melur, Madurai (Mad.)	Dumont 1957a
53	Paganeri, Ramanathapuram (Mad.)	Dumont 1957a
54	Mudukkulattur, Ramanathapuram (Mad.)	Dumont 1957a
55	Villages near Srivaikuntham, Tirunelveli (Mad.)	Dumont 1957a
56	Ramankara, Kottayam (Ker.)	Fuller 1976, 1978
57	Several villages, Palghat (Ker.)	Aiyappan 1937
58	Sakthikulangara and Neendaka, Quilon (Ker.)	Klausen 1968

[a]Numbers correspond to those in Figure 2.

tions in the role and status of Indian females, and as a demonstration of how anthropological expertise can be relevant to population and development policy.

Within the past decade there has been a growing interest among anthropologists in the relationship between culture and population. An excellent preliminary bibliography of some of the work inspired by this interest has been collected by Marshall, Morris, and Polgar (1972:268–278). One of the most fascinating areas of inquiry in the domain of population anthropology is that of cultural practices that seem to work against population growth. For many years scholars have been aware of cultural practices that tend to increase fertility, without realizing that many important features of culture have the opposite effect.

My book follows the lead of those who have pointed to social and cultural effects on population dynamics (Nag 1973; Ford 1964; Davis and Blake 1956) but extends the frontier by looking at the effect of

culture on both fertility and mortality in a complex hierarchical society. India, with its regional and social variation, provides a rich
laboratory for exploring the role of culture in population dynamics. In
that laboratory I have found that fatal female neglect can act as an
indigenous form of "family planning" which helps North Indians
adjust the sexual content of their families according to cultural dictates relating to production and property.

There have been some recent studies of indigenous means of
population regulation in primitive societies. Nag, in his review of
some of the problems and perspectives in population anthropology,
notes the lack of similar studies for peasant societies (1973:257–259).
Several articles in *Culture, Natality and Family Planning* (Marshall
and Polgar 1976) are steps toward reducing this gap in the literature
(Ascádi; Murray; Spring). The main weakness shared by these three
articles is that their authors extract one element such as ritual from the
entire sociocultural framework and proceed to try to demonstrate
that, for example, one specific ritual regulates population growth.
The reader is given not the slightest basis for understanding how the
control of population growth is related to other facts of life, a weakness from which I hope this work does not suffer.

Another important direction this volume pursues is the clarification
and delineation of the concept of "the Indian female." This term has
been too imprecisely used for too many years. The stereotype of "the
Indian female" as one of the world's most degraded and oppressed
creatures is erroneously based on a North Indian high caste model and
thus does not apply to all women in India. In the future, perhaps,
scholars will take more care in distinguishing between rich and poor
women, women of high caste and low caste, and women of the South
and women of the North. The stereotype is not completely wrong, but
its range of applicability must be sketched.

India is the first nation in the world to institute a national family
planning policy. India also has been the recipient of massive amounts
of family planning advice and aid from other countries though none
of this has been notably effective in solving what the Indian nation or
other nations view as India's "population problem."

This remarkable failure may be due in large part to the lack of
awareness on the part of planners of what Indian families themselves

think about family size and structure. Long before governments and private agencies began formulating population policies, the inhabitants of india were planning their families according to their own wishes and using a variety of methods.[6] That Indian peasants have their own ideas of family formation and "planning" has been overlooked by most experts, often to the detriment of these experts' sophisticated plans. They have wrongly assumed that rural Indians are, in terms of family planning, simply "empty vessels" waiting to be filled with knowledge of modern contraceptives (see Gould 1976 and Mamdani 1972). In fact, the vessels are not empty but are full of desires, preferences, and goals relating to both family size *and*, particularly in the North, its sexual composition.

Family planning experts are gradually becoming aware of the importance of son preference through a growing body of research on the subject, much of which has been done by anthropologists.[7] This research has led planners to the conclusion that son preference boosts fertility and is a powerful factor of resistance to national family planning objectives. The important fact thus far ignored by anthropologists and planners alike is that intense son preference is often coexistent with intense discrimination against daughters. Neglect of daughters and outright infanticide act not only to reduce the total number of daughters who survive, but also curb overall population growth by reducing the number of females who reach childbearing age and reproduce.

Development planners could utilize knowledge concerning this indigenous practice that, ironically enough, accomplishes some of the goals they support. A form of birth control which regulates the sex of offspring, while sometimes objected to in the United States on moral grounds, would find a wide audience of acceptors in rural India. Such a method, if proven safe for users, would solve many problems. The sufferings borne by unwanted daughters would end as would the impaired health of mothers who bear more children than they otherwise would if the birth of sons were more assured. Of course, there is

6. Mandelbaum (1974) discusses many cultural factors which affect family size and composition in India.

7. Williamson (1976, 1978) organizes a vast amount of cross-cultural evidence and reviews much of the recent literature on son preference.

the strong possibility that such a method would have the undesirable result of an even more drastic imbalancing of the sex ratio than now exists in northern India.

Beyond such an unpleasant and problematic solution as the one discussed above, the only other possibility with any long-range merit and no immediate large-scale problems attached is that of eliminating the bases of son preference and daughter discrimination—certainly no small task. One step in this direction would be to ensure increased rates of survival for children; parents would thus feel more assured that one or two sons are enough. Given the current high rates of child mortality, one must have five or six sons to feel assured that at least one will survive to maturity, or so the reasoning goes. Increased survival of sons would help to reduce the need to bear many children; thus it would reduce the number of unwanted daughters born in the quest for sons. Another tack would be to raise the status of exchange marriages and other forms of marriage which involve no great cost to the father of the bride. In this way one of the major burdens in raising several daughters would be erased from parents' minds. While neither of these steps gets at the true basis of the problem, inequality between males and females, they do offer a beginning toward its solution.

Another important implication of this study for development planners concerns the roles of females in production. While most developers are interested in keeping—or getting—women involved in production, development more often results in the further exclusion of females from the opportunity to work and earn. For example, in West Bengal, women formerly played a significant role in hulling rice from which they earned incomes (Fukutake et al. 1964:127). This task is now performed by machines; the women have no work to replace that which they have lost. This is modernization at its worst. The lesson is that any modernization effort should carefully consider its implications for female employment for, as this research shows, the very survival of the females affected may suffer.

There is a related aspect of female employment which is of interest to planners. The stereotype of the secluded, nonemployed Indian female is often taken as an important factor in creating high fertility levels. The reasoning is that if women have nothing else to do, they will have babies; if they work, they will be more apt to limit their reproductive capacity. This has been argued by Dixon (1978) who suggests that a solution to high fertility in countries where women are secluded is to remove those women from their homes and find them outside work. This suggestion has limited application to rural India because, as will be shown in Chapter 6, in many regions of India there is already a very high rate of female employment outside the home; women in much of Himalayan, Central, and South India are not sequestered within the home and the same is true for lower-class women all over India. Further, the assumption that secluded (and for the most part upper-class) women are more fertile than other women is still a highly debatable issue awaiting further investigation.

The last example of policy relevance illustrates the importance of looking beneath blanket statements such as "women in India are secluded" to find the regional and social differences. With this perspective, I have tried in my work to penetrate beneath broad facts and generalizations to find the crucial variations shrouded therein.

2
Nature, Culture, and the Proportions of the Sexes

Sex Ratios: Primary and Secondary

Given nature's equalizing tendencies, one would assume that the primary sex ratio, or sex ratio at the time of conception, would be roughly balanced. Cultural effects on primary sex ratio are difficult to imagine and, therefore, it seems logical that there would always be a fifty-fifty chance of either a boy or a girl being conceived. But this is not the case according to current research. What little is known about primary sex ratios derives mainly from studies done either on animal or on human embryos; studies of human embryos thus are the major source for this section.

Using human embryos to find out about primary sex ratios is not without its difficulties. First, embryos do not reveal what sex ratios are exactly at the time of *conception* since an embryo is usually several weeks or even months old before it can be studied and sexed with any degree of accuracy (Weir 1973:293). Second, most work with human embryos, obtained primarily through the performance of induced abortions, is done in the United States and other developed countries (Matthiessen and Matthiessen 1977; Yamamoto, Ito, and Watanabe 1977; Bochkov and Kostrova 1973; Lee and Takano 1970; Mikamo 1969).

Most findings indicate a high (preponderance of males) prenatal sex ratio. Lee and Takano (1970:1295) compare the results of ten studies of embryos obtained from both spontaneous and induced abortions in which sample size ranges from 125 cases to over 1,000, while age of the embryo varies from one to twenty-five weeks of gestational age. The sex ratios discovered were from a low of 60 (males per 100 females) to a high of 282 but the majority of the studies found high sex ratios (only three discovered a preponderance of females and all these were of very small numbers of cases). A separate study of 1,452 cases six to seven weeks old by Lee and Takano found a sex ratio of 153 (1970:1295). Using a different method of sex determination, Mikamo (1969) examined 736 embryos aged mainly one to three months. In the four age groups determined on the basis of embryo length, the sex ratios were (from youngest to oldest) 63.6, 108.5, 125.4, and 126.9, giving an average of 107.3 (1969:274). It is noteworthy that the only preponderantly female sex ratio was at the earliest stage of development when the difficulty of sexing the embryo is greatest.

Admittedly, the study of primary or prenatal sex ratios is at a very crude level of development. Nothing can be said with surety: samples are often small, embryos under five months of age are difficult to sex with accuracy, and theories remain highly speculative. Most scholars feel that the sex ratio right at the time of conception is extremely unbalanced toward males and that the imbalance gradually declines throughout gestation. This decline is assumed to occur mainly be- cause the male embryo is less hardy than the female embryo, and more often aborts spontaneously. (The difference in viability between male and female fetuses has yet to be explained.) Therefore, through- out the duration of conception, more male fetuses than female are lost, resulting in a less dramatic preponderance of males at the time of birth. This pattern of greater fetal wastage of males is reaffirmed by the high sex ratio of stillborn babies (Stevenson and Bobrow 1967), perhaps due to the greater birth stress males suffer as a result of their larger size (Stern 1960).

There are many studies and reports on the secondary sex ratio, or sex ratio at birth, in humans, but again these largely concern popula- tions in the developed countries. The most reliable are based on long-term recording of hospital births. Less reliable but more easily obtainable are censuses and other official reports. Inaccuracies in these latter sources stem from simple error and inability to keep track of people who usually give birth outside of hospitals. There is also the possibility that misreporting is based on cultural conceptions concerning which births are worth recording.

No doubt the United States has one of the most efficient and accurate systems for recording sex ratios at birth, for most babies in the U.S. are born in hospitals, and recording of birth is required by law. The sex ratio at birth for the United States is 105.5 (U.N. 1976). This figure is often taken as a "norm" against which other countries' sex ratios at birth are judged. The assumption that the overall sex ratio at birth for the U.S. is *the standard* is certainly more than ethnocentric; it may be inaccurate, too. Even the fact that sex ratios at birth in other nations with highly developed census-keeping operations also tend to hover around 105 is still no reason to suppose that 105 is the "right" sex ratio.

One study of the range of sex ratios at birth from 76 countries with relatively dependable census registration provides an idea of how wide the diversity is: from a low of 90.2 in Montserrat to a high of 116.2 in the Gambia. Visaria, who analyzes these data, explains: "Several of the values are based on a small number of births and admit of a nonnegligible [*sic*] random error. However, 50 out of 80 values fall within the usually stated range of sex ratio at birth—104–107 (inclusive). . . . Of the 30 deviant values of sex ratios at birth, 23 fall below the lower limit of the usual range (104) and 7 exceed the upper limit of 107" (1967*b*:133). How Visaria arrives at "the usually stated range" of 104 to 107 is not explained. Perhaps it is impossible to delineate such a range at this stage but, just as a rule of thumb, I would extend Visaria's lower limit to 102. In this way there are 10 values falling below the lower limit and 7 above. Of course this is not a scientifically derived standard either, but, given the state of knowledge, it seems better to opt for a wider (102–107) than a narrower (104–107) range.

As mentioned above, the most dependable data on sex ratio at birth come from hospital records of large numbers of births. A few examples of these are worth examining.[1] Records for 9,070 births in Addis

---

1. I did not systematically search for such reports, since variation in sex ratio at birth, while an interesting subject, does not seem to be the reason behind sex ratio imbalances in the Indian population as discussed in Chapter 4 and Appendix A.

Ababa show a sex ratio of 105.8, which is within the broad range of expectability (Gebre-Medhin, Gurovsky, and Bondestam 1976). Two other examples are of unusually high sex ratios. In a district of Java, the sex ratio of infants born in the hospital during 1954–1958 was found to be 118 (Timmer 1961:191). The size of the sample is not given, though it must be quite large as the period covered by the study was four years. Another very masculine sex ratio was found in over ten thousand births that occurred in ten hospitals in South Korea during 1956–1960; the sex ratio of these births was 116.9 (Kang and Cho 1962). In commenting upon this Korean sex ratio, Visaria notes: "The 95% confidence limits for this sex ratio are 112.66–121.39 and even the lower limit is considerably removed from the upper limit of 107 of the usual range. Thus, until contrary evidence emerges, Korea must be accepted, provisionally, as an instance of an abnormally high sex ratio" (1967b:141).

More and better evidence is greatly needed; perhaps other Korean studies may well prove this high sex ratio of 116.9 to be atypical for Korea. Reports of small numbers of births recorded on the basis of hearsay should in general be viewed with strong skepticism. Such a report is Beckerman's of a sex ratio at birth of 185 for 77 live births in a village in Ecuador (1976). In such a small population, a very high sex ratio at birth is a statistical possibility; however, in this instance I would not rule out the possibility, as the author does, of female infanticide. Census reports must also be treated with care, as sex selection may be a distorting factor, a point that Visaria (1967b:140–141) makes for Egyptian data and that also applies to India.

On the basis of all reports and studies examined here, it is apparent that males tend slightly to outnumber females at birth. However, we are very far indeed from having a dependable and detailed picture of secondary sex ratios worldwide and any explanations for variations that appear to exist are only tentative.

Infancy and Infanticide

While biology is largely responsible for variations in primary and secondary sex ratios, sex ratios later in the life cycle are more clearly under the influence of culture. Common sense leads one to assume that from birth both sexes have an equal chance of survival except, of course, for maternity and its accompanying hazards which only females experience. But equality is rarely the case.

There is a current saying that "females are the biologically superior sex" which many people believe and which seems, to a certain point, accurate (Newland 1979). The higher attrition rate of male fetuses and the higher stillborn rate for males stand as potential evidence, as does the higher death rate of male infants in the first year of life in Western nations. Indeed, at age one, the proportion of the sexes is equal in the West; it seems that nature has "stacked the deck" in favor of males at the time of conception, knowing the frailty of males, simply so that things could even out later on. However, the balance is not maintained for long, though it is sometimes difficult to sort out whether it is culture or nature (or the interplay of both) that is responsible. There is, however, some stark evidence from many cultures demonstrating the power of culture to define which will be the "superior" sex in terms of survival. One of the clearest instances of this is sex-selective infanticide.

Infanticide has long attracted the attention and horror of Western travelers, missionaries, and anthropologists, but its capacity to alter sex ratios, or population growth, has only recently been subjected to careful scrutiny. In spite of the interest in the subject, broad comparative studies are rare. There are one anthropological survey (Williamson 1978), two brief historical surveys (Langer 1973; Radbill 1968), and a good bibliography which includes sources on both simple and complex societies (Dickeman 1975). Apthekar's classic *Anjea* (1931) is a collection of many examples of infanticide, as diverse as the Viking practice of exposing infants and the female infanticide of the polyandrous South India Todas. Apthekar was one of the earliest writers to suggest that infanticide can function as a mechanism of population control. More recently, Divale and Harris (Divale 1970; Divale and Harris 1976) have developed a theory that, for primitive societies at least, links warfare and female infanticide together as the major components of a population-growth regulating system.[2] There are several more sharply focused anthropological studies of infanti-

2. This is not to say that I completely accept Divale and Harris's theory that explains female infanticide as part of a population regulating system in conjunction with warfare. The distribution of female infanticide, even within primitive societies,

cide such as Freeman (1971) and Balikçi (1967) on the Eskimo, Divale (1971) on the Ibo, and Granzberg (1973) on twin infanticide.

Many excellent historical studies of infanticide have been done for a narrow time period and area: fourteenth- and fifteenth-century Florence (Trexler 1973), feudal and post-Restoration Japan (Bowles 1953), the later Middle Ages in England (Kellum 1973), and tenth-century France (Coleman 1974). Piers's recent work, entitled *Infanticide* (1978) provides many examples, also mainly from Europe, but the reader is distracted by her attempts at a psychological explanation (that is, weak object-attachment of the mother to the child). Dickeman (1976) presents a most interesting analysis of historical data from India, China, and Florence in her construction of the relationship between dowry-hypergamy marriages and the killing of daughters. Much of the evidence from the above sources again points to preferential female infanticide, though the European pattern has yet to be clearly depicted.

The best of the historical studies is Smith's *Nakahara: Family Farming and Population in a Japanese Village, 1717–1830* (1977). Smith carefully analyzes voluminous census records and comes to the conclusion that Nakaharans practiced a sort of "family planning" which was integrally related to the needs of agricultural production such that children not "needed" were killed. While the author found evidence of male infanticide (generally later-born males), female infanticide was preponderant.

In order to obtain an idea of the extent of the practice of female infanticide in primitive groups cross-culturally, the reader should refer to Divale and Harris (1976) who have employed data on juvenile sex ratios for over three hundred societies. In spite of criticisms concerning the data employed (Hirschfeld, Howe, and Levin 1978), it cannot be denied that the data demonstrate that the practice of female infanticide is very widespread throughout primitive society and that its effects within such societies are demographically significant.

One thing is clear from most studies: systematic infanticide,

---

is far more widespread than is warfare; therefore any causal connection between infanticide and warfare is partial at best. Examples of primitive societies that practice female infanticide but not warfare are some Australian bands and many Eskimo groups; examples from peasant societies can also easily be recognized.

wherever it is practiced, Europe or the South Seas, is directed primarily toward females. Although one can find cases of sporadic male infanticide in the literature, or of infanticide that is not sex selective, the preponderant number of cases involve females. *Systematic* male infanticide is extremely rare; *systematic* female infanticide appears almost endemic among some peoples. What does this indicate for the present inquiry into the effects of culture on the proportions of the sexes?

First, culture provides the motivations for infanticide, whether they are seen by the people involved as ritualistic (Benedict 1972:80), economic (Granzberg 1973), or ecological (Freeman 1971). It is culture that "invents" the reasons for which some children who are born are not desired. Second, it is culture that sketches the outlines of the group that is to be the target of infanticide: whether it is to be only boys, only girls, first sons, daughters beyond the first, children born on Thursday, children born with teeth, or children with crippling deformities. Exactly *why* a certain target group is named within any culture cannot be answered, for in many cases it may be purely arbitrarily assigned. However, if infanticide, particularly of females, is practiced frequently, then the possibility looms large that its occurrence may have significant demographic repercussions, whether or not those consequences are recognized and valued by the groups involved.

Childhood and Neglect

In glaring contradiction to those who, with LeVine (1977:20), hold that one of the universal goals of parents vis-à-vis their children is the "physical survival and health of the child," we have seen that some parents opt for the termination of the life of their child through infanticide. However, a child's life can also be shortened through the more subtle effects of child abuse and neglect (CA/N).

Child abuse and neglect includes a wide range of behavior which is difficult to typologize with any exactitude, especially if one wishes to make the typology usable cross-culturally. First, it is helpful to distinguish forms of neglect from those of abuse. I view the two as different in that abuse is more "active" in the way it is inflicted; it is abuse when something is actually *done* to harm the child. In the case of neglect, harm comes to the child because something is *not done* which should have been. Thus sexual molestation of a child is abusive, whereas depriving a child of adequate food and exercise is neglectful. One similarity between neglect and abuse is that both, if carried far enough, can be fatal.

The history of public concern with CA/N is short and is limited to the Western world at this stage (Radbill 1968). Most research now being done is focused on the situation "at home," with little concern to view the problem globally. More work is being done by child development experts and psychologists than anthropologists, unfortunately; the only cross-cultural research on the subject of which I am aware is Rohner's (1975).Compared with the level of anthropological research on infanticide, that on child neglect and abuse is an even greater wasteland, all the more shocking because child abuse and neglect are no doubt much more widespread—indeed, CA/N is probably a cultural universal.

Although some researchers have undertaken functional analyses of infanticide, neglect is rarely mentioned in connection with other population-regulating factors (Benedict 1972; Douglas 1966; Ford 1964; Nag 1968; Davis and Blake 1956), though infanticide usually receives a paragraph or two. Harris, in his text *People, Culture and Nature*, provides an exception to this generalization; he delineates several forms of infanticide: homicide, malign aggression, and conscious and unconscious neglect (1975:258). Neglect, however, is not properly a subtype of infanticide as it is not always fatal. In fact, I would rather categorize infanticide as a subtype of child abuse and neglect, at the extreme end of the continuum at which it becomes fatal.

References to neglect occasionally surface when an author is discussing another subject. Prothro's work on child-rearing practices in Lebanon is such an instance. He first notes an imbalance in the ratio of boys to girls in the areas where he studied: ". . . in Beirut and in the valley the number of living male children in the household exceeds the number of females by about one-fifth. In Beirut it is possible that this sex ratio can be explained in part by the fact that young girls may work away from home as servants. Such an explanation cannot apply to valley villages" (1967:15).

Prothro cites another scholar who studied in Lebanon, Churchill, who explains the discrepancy in the sex ratio as being due to differential survival rates for boys and girls based on comparative neglect of female children; this cue alerted Prothro subsequently to search for possible sexual discrimination while making his study. His sample consists of 468 children (247 boys, 221 girls) at the age of five years which yields a sex ratio of 111, or one similar to that of the entire Lebanese juvenile population (1967:46).

Being aware of the strong preference for sons in Lebanon, Prothro asked whether male children are treated with greater warmth than female children (1967:66). He found that, according to his indicators, boys do in fact receive more warmth than girls. He also examined duration of breast feeding for both sexes and discovered that boys are consistently breast-fed for a longer time than girls (1967:74). While neither of these findings is conclusive evidence of greater *mortality* related to discrimination in the allocation of warmth or breast milk, there is a strong possibility that Prothro has discovered aspects of a culture of son preference coupled with discrimination against daughters very similar to what can be found in North India.

A few more examples of neglect, again involving relative neglect of females as compared with males, are worth considering here. According to Adams (1976) who studied the Barama River Carib, Carib women are consistently less well nourished than Carib men. This differential begins in childhood when girls are denied access to the jungle where boys are allowed to go and where the boys then have access to "casual" sources of protein. The female population is thus from youth weaker than the male, a fact that is especially critical during periods of food shortage, as females have less resistance to disease. Outright female infanticide among the Carib has also been reported by the same author (1972:69–71).

Sex differentials in mortality due to famines and epidemics are a particularly interesting area of inquiry. Just as among the Carib, it has been found that during epidemics in China, the death rate of girls is higher than that of boys (Lang 1946:150). Again, this occurrence has been ascribed to the lower nutritional status of girls which renders them less resistant to disease. A strong cultural preference for sons in China is probably at the root of both the lower nutritional standard of girls and their higher mortality rates during epidemics.

A fascinating study of how culture works to create a particular sex pattern of mortality during a famine has been done by Greenough (1977; forthcoming 1982). A large part of his *Prosperity and Misery in Modern Bengal: The Bengal Famine of 1943–1944* (1982) is devoted to a lengthy presentation of age and sex patterns of "victimization." Victimization is defined as being "the sum of the processes by which certain persons are deprived of their expected life conditions or of life itself. . . ." Using records of the Bengal famine relief committee, Greenough found that during the 1943–1944 famine in West Bengal, victimization occurred in a patterned fashion: certain age and sex groups fared consistently worse than others. Adult males aged 20–40 years had the lowest mortality rates, a fact Greenough finds consistent with cultural emphasis on the maintenance of the *korta*, or head of the family. Females aged 15–20 years had higher rates of mortality but still compare favorably to other segments of the population, especially the very old of both sexes who fared the worst. An important feature of the juvenile death rates is that for both the 1–5 and the 5–10 categories, girls have higher mortality rates than boys. The conclusion may be drawn that, given a harsh economic situation dictated by famine, cultural rules about who are the most valued members of the family come into play. These rules demand that able-bodied males be nourished first, then able-bodied females. Children are less valued than adults and, among these, girls are less valued than boys. While economic hardship determines that some people must die, it is culture that dictates who are to be victims.[3]

It must be remembered that systematic neglect of certain children does not happen during famines, epidemics, or other "emergency" situations. It can also be prevalent in "normal" conditions, as Prothro's (1976) findings demonstrate.

Future research may prove that systematic child neglect, like infanticide, is more often directed toward females than males. Because of the scant number of studies of neglect available at this stage, any

3. Although Greenough (1978) has cautioned me that his explanation of victimization has not been unanimously accepted, I feel that such resistance must be based more on emotion than careful thought. Greenough has used large amounts of data, carefully drawn together cultural facts, and woven what is to my mind a most convincing argument.

generalization is highly tenuous. The important point for academics and planners is that, when they study or attempt to change child-care practices, differentials based on the child's sex may be critical. Before differences in attitudes toward and treatment of the sexes can be changed, they must be acknowledged.

Discrimination against females continues beyond the childhood years. There is evidence that females *as a group* can be viewed as "neglected." A recent study (Preston 1976) on sex differences in the cause of death throughout the world reveals that diarrhea is the predominant medical cause of death among females, particularly in Third World countries. There are several forms of diarrhea which can be fatal, but most tend to be precipitated and severely aggravated by poor nutrition. The possibility arises that, in general, females worldwide are less well nourished and well cared for than males. If this is the case, anthropologists might well investigate the cultural underpinnings of discrimination against females in specific situations. Planning programs that attempt to ameliorate nutritional standards should take into account existing differentials within a group or community and should be cognizant of the values motivating these differentials. Knowledge of who the victims are is indispensable in any attempt at de-victimization.

3
Female Infanticide
in British India

One of the most striking aspects of the history of female infanticide in India is the lack of reticence on the part of Indians to admit to the murdering of their female offspring—that is, before the British outlawed infanticide in 1870 and began to take steps to enforce the law.[1] For example, such reports as the one quoted below are quite common; here the nineteenth-century British official Sleeman notes the reply given him by a landholder in Uttar Pradesh when asked whether he thought that evil comes from murdering female infants:

'No, Sir, I do not.'—'But the greater part of the Rajpoot families do still murder them, do they not?' 'Yes, Sir, they still destroy them; and we believe, that the father who preserves a daughter will never live to see her suitably married, or, that the family into which she does marry, will perish or be ruined.' 'Do you recollect any instances of this?' 'Yes, Sir, my uncle Dureeao, preserved a daughter, but died before he could see her married; and my father was obliged to go to the cost of getting her married into a Chouhan family, at Mynpooree, in the British territory. My grandfather, Nathoo, and his brother, Rughonath, preserved each a daughter, and married them into the same Chouhan families of Mynpooree. These families all became ruined,

1. This contrasts with the expected situation in which the murder of infants would be a very hushed-up practice. Aginsky, for example, could elicit no information on infanticide from the Shanel Pomo tribe of California even though he was sure it was practiced (1939). It is possible, though, that such reticence is the product of contact with disapproving Westerners, as it was in North India.

and their lands were sold by auction; and the three women returned
upon us, one having two sons and a daughter; and another two sons—
we maintained them for some years with difficulty; but this year,
seeing the disorder that prevailed around us, they all went back to the
families of their husbands.—It is the general belief among us, Sir, that
those who preserve their daughters never prosper; and, that the families into which we marry them are equally unfortunate.' 'Then you
think that it is a duty imposed upon you from above, to destroy your
infant daughters; and that the neglect and disregard of that duty brings
misfortunes upon you?' 'We think it must be so, Sir, with regard to
our own families or clan!' [Reeves 1971:279]

In spite of the relative ease and openness with which the subject of
female infanticide was regarded in India, the historic record contains
more anecdotal evidence than quantitative documentation. However,
by combining official reports with data from the earliest Indian censuses, one can partially reconstruct the social context and demographic significance of female infanticide in British times.

Discovery and Suppression

The first discovery of female infanticide occurred in 1789 among the
Rajkumar clan of Rajputs in Jaunpur District, eastern Uttar Pradesh;
an official named Jonathan Duncan is attributed with this finding.
Previously, foreign observers assumed that the apparent scarcity of
females in northern India was due to the invisibility of those females.
As one indefatigable traveler, Fanny Parks, comments in her
nineteenth-century diary: "I have been nearly four years in India and
never beheld any women, but those in attendance as servants in
European families, the low caste wives of petty shopkeepers and nach
[dancing] women" (Parks 1975, I:59). The girls and women, it was
believed, existed—they were just hidden from view because of the
requirements of the purdah system. While seclusion of females is part
of the basis of Parks's consternation, it is also true that there were not
as many women as men *in existence*.

The course that a few dedicated British officials followed in discovering and attempting to suppress female infanticide in their various districts is reported by Panigrahi (1976). She describes in vivid
detail the history of its discovery, using reports such as the following
to emphasize the immensity of the problem:

> James Thomason accidentally discovered the practice [of female in-
> fanticide] in 1835, while he was engaged in revising the settlements of
> the Deogaon and Nizamabad parganas in Azamgarh. . . . In conversa-
> tion with some of the zamindars . . . he happened to refer to one of
> them as the son-in-law of another. This mistake raised a sarcastic
> laugh among them and a bystander briefly explained that he could not
> be a son-in-law since there were no daughters in the village. Thoma-
> son was told that the birth of a daughter was considered a most serious
> calamity and she was seldom allowed to live. No violent measures
> were however resorted to, but she was left to die from neglect and
> want of food. [Panigrahi 1976:20–21]

Reports of other villages and "tribes" without even *one* female child
increased until finally the British government began to take an interest.
One hundred years after the official discovery of female infanticide in
India, the Infanticide Act of 1870 was passed, abolishing its practice. In
1881 a Special Census Report on Sex Statistics in the Northwestern
Provinces and Oudh was undertaken which showed a great scarcity of
females there (Pakrasi 1970).

Arousing concern about female infanticide was not difficult, but there
were barriers of a political nature in the way of its suppression. The
general attitude of the British toward Rajputs and other "manly" groups
of northern India was inhibiting, and it was such people as these who
were mainly guilty of practicing infanticide. Panigrahi describes the
situation: "The British government respected the Rajputs for their past
glory, gallantry, sense of honour and honesty. Many eulogistic
anecdotes about them gained currency at this time and are still
well-known. Hence the British Residents, although powerful in their
dominions, allowed them considerable freedom in their administration
as compared to other Indian states" (1976:30).

While strong measures were taken to prohibit the practice of suttee
(widow burning) and to stamp out thuggee (gang robbery and murder), little effort was made to eradicate female infanticide.[2] The gov-
ernor-general of India, Lord William Bentinck, himself admitted
that if suttee had been practiced to a great degree by the bold people
of the Northern Provinces he would have been hesitant in passing a
proclamation against it (Panigrahi 1970:45). Indeed, respect for the
Rajputs was coupled with fear of them, for they were scarcely securely

---

2. For an account of suttee, see Stein (1978); for the story of the suppression of
thuggee, see Bruce (1968).

contained under the control of the British: "The fact was that the Rajputs were a martial race and they formed the bulk of the Indian army.
In Oudh they were in a chronic state of rebellion. . . . Therefore political exigencies dictated that nothing should be done to offend their
sensibilities, and that safeguards had to be created against the over-
enthusiastic proceedings of young and energetic officials of the Government" (Panigrahi 1976:145). Concerned with keeping the peace,
the Government invoked the "inviolability of the home." Even when
confronted with such glaring evidence as that presented by Burnes
(1834) about the Rajputs of Gujarat, reporting that among the infanticidal Rajput groups in that province there were counted 815
boys and 144 girls, the Government replied in the following way:

> I have perused with attention the report on Hindu Infanticide in Cutch,
> by Mr. Burnes. . . . It is clear that this system cannot be abolished by
> preventive measures of police. A system of domiciliary *espionage*
> might be prepared to watch over individual cases of birth, and to warn
> the parents against the destruction of the gift of God, but such an
> expedient would be of very doubtful advantage. It is a remedy against
> evil which has never been adopted by the East Indian government; it is
> one which would degrade the practisers of it, and be revolting to those
> subjected to it; and if there is any one cause which has more than
> another contributed to the establishment and security of our Indian
> empire, it is the inviolability of the subject's roof, and the absence of
> all scrutiny in his domestic concerns. [Burnes 1834:193–194]

Ultimately the British, after the East India company ceded control
to the crown, resorted to a variety of measures in the attempt to
induce people to keep their daughters alive. There were conferences
held on the evils of infanticide, establishment of dowry funds with
government money to help fathers pay for the marriages of daughters
they preserved, threats of imprisonment and fines, and friendly
cajoling.[3] Success was slow. Raikes, district collector of Mainpuri,
western Uttar Pradesh, reports on one example of success which must
have swelled his predecessor Unwin's heart with almost grandfather-

3. An interesting historical tidbit is a diagram of the seating arrangement at
the Amritsar conference, October 31, 1853, for which see Cave-Browne 1857:
Appendix, n.p. The conference brought together several dozen caste leaders
from North India to discuss possible solutions for the problem of female infanticide.

ly pride, for Unwin himself had barely escaped murder by angry Rajputs of the district when he tried to suppress infanticide there:

> There is at Mynpoorie an old fortress, which looks far over the valley of the Eesun river. This has been for centuries the stronghold of the Rajahs of Mynpoorie, Chohans whose ancient blood, descending from the great Pirthee Raj and the regal stem of Neemrana, represents *la creme de la creme* of Rajpoot aristocracy. Here when a son, a nephew, a grandson was born to the reigning chief, the event was announced to the neighboring city by the loud discharge of wall-pieces and match-locks; but centuries had passed away and no infant daughter had been known to smile within those walls.
>
> In 1845, however, thanks to the vigilance of Mr. Unwin, a little grand-daughter was preserved by the Rajah of that day. The fact was duly notified to the Government and a letter of congratulation and a dress of honour were at once dispatched from headquarters to the Rajah. [Raikes 1852:20]

Events such as this were repeated throughout northern India. British officials became convinced that infanticide was, if not completely stamped out, well on its way toward extinction.

Who Practiced Female Infanticide?

One fact clearly emerges from the welter of reports and secondary studies from British India: female infanticide was not universally practiced. That is, it was not practiced in every region of India, and not everyone in those areas was involved.

Regionally the practice of female infanticide was confined mainly to the northern part of India from Gujarat in the west to the eastern border of present-day Uttar Pradesh (Fig. 3). A scanning of Buchanan's writings (Oldham 1930) on Bihar produced no information on infanticide in that state, which lies directly east of Uttar Pradesh. Yet it seems strange that the practice would abate so abruptly at the Bihar border. The only example of infanticide from northeastern India is that of the tribal Nagas. Examples from the area south of the Central Provinces (Madhya Pradesh today) are few: the Todas of the Nilgiri Hills in the state of Madras; mention of its occurrence in Vizakhapatnam District of the present state of Andhra Pradesh (Thurston 1975:504); and the tribal Khonds of what is now mostly Koraput

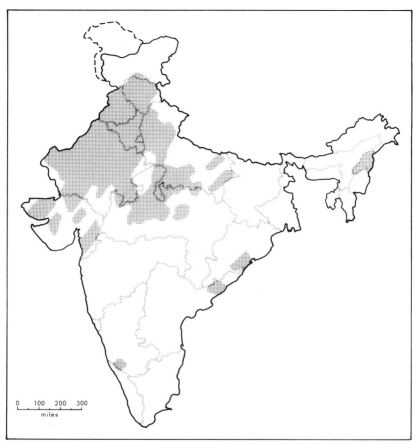

Figure 3 Generalized areas of female infanticide in British India according to secondary sources. Sources: Burnes (1834); *Calcutta Review* (1844); Cave-Browne (1857); Das (1956); Das (1957); Hecht (1972); Nath (1973); O'Dwyer (1925); Oldham (1930); Pakrasi (1968); Pakrasi and Sasmal (1971); Raikes (1852); Reeves (1971); Risley (1969); Thurston (1975); Tod (1971). Note: Only the present territory of independent India is shown.

District in the state of Orissa (O'Malley 1975:94). These scattered examples of infanticide outside North India are provocative cases demanding their own explanation. As I have not examined any of them in a systematic way, I can offer only the suggestion that these groups, like so many other infanticidal tribal groups, as compared with infanticidal peasants, practiced infanticide primarily because of its "family planning" effects.

From all reports available, it is clear that female infanticide in nineteenth-century India was practiced primarily in the higher social groups of the North, though this point is debatable. Dickeman, for instance, questions the assignment of female infanticide to only up-per-level castes, suggesting that low-caste people simply were not studied by the British (1976:2). This suggestion seems unlikely, though, if one reads Cave-Browne (1857) who cites quite detailed census information and in general is very careful in differentiating among various groups who did and did not practice infanticide. No doubt, in the North, the problem is one of degree: it could be that in the most infanticide-endemic areas, all castes practiced it to some extent, but it was clearly the higher social groups who were most extreme, preserving no daughters at all.

One of the earliest official sources of information on female infan-ticide can be consulted usefully at this juncture. The 1881 Northwest Provinces Special Census Report named seven caste groups as the most "suspected" castes: Jats, Gujars, Tagas, Ahars, Rajputs, Minas, and Ahirs (Pakrasi 1970:87). These are all middle- and upper-level castes.

In other areas of northern India, groups that appear prominently in the literature as infanticidal are also of the upper level, generally landed and therefore relatively wealthy. In addition to Rajputs, who receive almost ubiquitous mention, notable examples include the Sikhs of the Punjab (Cave-Browne 1857:112), Khatris of northwest-ern India, Kanbis of Gujarat (Nath 1973:386), and Muslim Pathans of the Punjab (Cave-Browne 1857:127).

I have found only one reference to Brahmans, Moyal Brahmans of Punjab, practicing outright infanticide (Cave-Browne 1857:125). Re-cently Tambiah has stated that, while Rajputs were notorious for practicing female infanticide, Brahmans refrained from doing so be-cause they are "devoted to the practise of non-violence and vegetar-ianism" (1973:67). But, in spite of their dietary proclivities, there is little doubt that certain northern Brahmans are currently guilty of neglecting some of their daughters to death.

Motivations

Observers of the situation in British India were not loath to offer explanations for the practice of female infanticide. There was surprisingly little disagreement as to the reasons behind female infanticide. They were, briefly, "pride and purse," or the practice of hypergamy and the necessity of giving large dowries.[4] Pride of blood prompted a father to marry his daughter only to a family with status at least equal to, preferably higher than, that of his own. The payment of a large dowry was the only way to secure a husband of such a high status family. In this regard Crooke poetically noted at the end of the nineteenth century that the giving of large dowries "seriously cripples the resources of a man whose quiver is full of daughters" (1971:136). As a result of the financial burden of marrying off a daughter on one hand and the unbearable shame and danger of having an unmarried nubile daughter still at home on the other, families chose to murder these troublesome creatures at birth.

A recent attempt to explain female infanticide in demographic terms incorporates the ideas of pride and purse into a sociobiological framework. In her paper "Infanticide and Hypergamy: A Neglected Relationship," Dickeman argues that infanticide must be studied in a relation to "general theories of mammalian social reproductive systems, as an instance of . . . the maintenance of demographic structures necessary to the survival of the population" (1976:1). Dickeman views hypergamy as working genetically to improve the population involved, arguing that, due to the (unproven) scarcity of females at the bottom of the marriage hierarchy of hypergamous groups, there must be less breeding at these lower levels. Since the author apparently correlates low economic status with undesirable, less viable genes, she can then infer from this that reduced breeding in the lower echelons works to improve the quality of the genes in the whole population. This situation contrasts with that at the top of the marriage hierarchy. Men in the upper status level have access to more women through not only polygyny but also concubinage (1976:5), thus the desirable genes of the men at the top have better chances of

4. Many writers even now subscribe to this explanation (Majumdar 1954; Pakrasi 1968; Minturn and Hitchcock 1966:58).

spreading throughout the population and apparently enriching the quality of the genes thereof. She sees dowry as "a crucial link between sociocultural systems and the operation of natural selection in man" (1976:12). Dowry is a mark of economic success which becomes translated into reproductive terms.

Such a sociobiological explanation of female infanticide is inadequate for many reasons. First, it rests on unproven assumptions such as the one that people of high economic standing have genes that are more conducive to the survival of the population than do people who are poor. Second, this approach fails to help explain the presence of infanticide in areas where the ideological contrivances of hypergamy and dowry are not at work and there is no apparent "upward" flow of genes.

The unanimous interest of writers in the motivations of pride and purse are indicative of the importance to which Indians themselves ascribe these factors: pride and purse form a major portion of the emic perspective, of the ideology involved.[5] Certainly this is an important part of a wider system, but it is only one part. For a fuller understanding of the total system of female infanticide in British India one would need information on production, the sexual division of labor, property and its allocation, the distribution of power, and so forth. Only with such information can the ideology involving pride and purse be put into perspective, for pride and purse as ideological elements are not arbitrary, but are systematically related to material facts of life.

British officials who discovered the practice of infanticide area by area and caste by caste had a different perspective from that of most of the census commissioners, though often former district officers, like Risley, later became census writers. District officers Duncan, Unwin, and Montgomery talked to rajas and peasants alike about infanticide, its motivations, and its very methods, in great detail. Census writers, on the other hand, were confronted with the returns giving sex distributions within the population under their jurisdiction

5. A modern example of reliance on the emic interpretation to the exclusion of other explanatory factors is Hecht's study of female infanticide in nineteenth-century North India (1972). She discounts the possibility that infanticide might be related to "population control" as the latter does not form part of the emic record.

and then had to set about explaining any peculiar situations. Infanticide in India had been outlawed and almost forgotten by the time that regular Indian censuses began being published. Nevertheless certain keen observers of Indian society like Crooke were well aware that if outright infanticide had been suppressed, it had been supplanted by its more subtle form, neglect:

> The actual murder of little girls has in a great measure ceased, but it has been replaced in some tribes by a degree of carelessness hardly less criminal. It is found in some districts that, when fever is prevalent, girls' deaths, especially in the first three years of life, so largely exceed those of males that it is impossible not to believe that but small attempts are made to save the girls, and in many places deaths caused by disease of the lungs or malnutrition suggest the same conclusion. [Crooke 1971:138]

Yet it seems, from reading the census reports, that most other observers were more than willing to minimize the importance of either infanticide or neglect in explaining the sex ratio disparities that did indeed appear in census counts.

The 1872 Census

In the General Report (1872:13) it is stated that in all of British India the population comprised 98 million males and 92 million females, giving a sex ratio of 106.4 (males per 100 females). The adult sex ratio was about 101.0; the juvenile sex ratio, that is, of children under twelve, was 114.8. The proportion of adults to children was approximately 100 adults to 54 children.[6]

Table 2 displays juvenile and adult sex ratios for the provinces of British India in 1872. The juvenile sex ratios presented are all over 100; only in the southern states of Mysore and Madras are they within the range of expectability. Bengal, surprisingly, has a sex ratio as masculine as that of the notoriously infanticidal Northwest Provinces;

---

6. The reason for mentioning the adult-child proportion is that, according to Kelly (1975:34), since the sex ratio at birth may be slightly masculine, then a large proportion of children in the population would logically produce a higher overall sex ratio. The difference, however, would be of only slight magnitude.

Table 2

Males per 100 females in British India, juveniles and adults, by province, 1872

Province	Juvenile sex ratio[a]	Adult sex ratio	Overall sex ratio
Bengal[b]	120.1	90.7	99.8
Assam	116.2	101.0	106.4
Mysore	103.1	99.4	100.7
Madras	104.1	98.8	101.0
Central Provinces	108.6	99.8	103.5
Berar[c]	112.8	103.8	107.0
Oude[d]	118.6	102.3	107.8
Bombay	111.8	108.9	109.9
Northwest Provinces	120.1	103.8	114.2
Punjab[e]	118.6	120.3	119.7
Coorg[f]	108.3	138.8	127.9
Ajmere	—	—	201.7

Source: India 1875:13–14.
[a]Juvenile refers to the population under 12 years of age; adults are all those 12 years and above.
[b]Bengal includes, approximately, what is now West Bengal, Bihar, Orissa, and Bangladesh.
[c]Berar is located in what is now northern Maharashtra.
[d]Oude forms much of the eastern section of what is now Uttar Pradesh.
[e]Punjab at this time was undivided and comprised areas in Pakistan and Northwest India.
[f]The very masculine adult sex ration in Coorg, southern India, is apparently due to large influxes of male plantation labor.

this is a mystery which I cannot now solve.[7] Besides Bengal, provinces with extremely high juvenile sex ratios in 1872 are in the North: Oudh, the Northwest Provinces, and Punjab. Census writers were struck by the variation in sex ratios between provinces. The General Report of the census summarizes some of the explanations proposed; they are worth quickly reviewing here.

Sex ratio at birth was invoked as early as this census as an explanation for later high sex ratios. Two of the major factors believed to

7. If the 1872 census data for Bengal were accepted as accurate, then it would be a great puzzle as to how and why the sex ratio changed from 120.1 (for the under-twelve population of what then included present West Bengal, Bihar, Orissa, and Bangladesh) to its present pattern of female preponderance in the under-ten rural population: the range of all West Bengal districts in the 1961 Census extends from a low of 970 males per 1,000 females to a high of 1,002. However, there is some reason to question the 1872 figure as later censuses show Bengal (in its various shapes) to have quite low juvenile sex ratios.

produce more males at birth were the effects of a hot climate and the young age at which girls were married; the greater maturity of the husband supposedly lent greater strength to the "male element," resulting in the birth of more male babies. However, no one has ever demonstrated any correlation between climate, marriage age, and sex ratio (it would probably be impossible). And, furthermore, sex ratio at birth as reported by the 1872 Census was, for all of India, only very slightly male: male births were *1 percent* higher than female births (General Report 1875:13). A 1 percent male advantage at birth can scarcely provide an explanation for juvenile sex ratios as unbalanced as those in the Northwest. It is a pity that census writers did not give more credence to this fact; it would have saved a lot of time and paper later, for even today sex ratios at birth are still proposed as explanation for unbalanced sex ratios.

The other favorite explanation is inaccuracies in the census: "Perhaps the excess of males is to a large extent only apparent, being due either to the omission of females owing to the low estimation in which they are held, or to their systematic concealment in consequence of the reticence practiced in an Oriental country on all matters connected with female relations" (General Report 1875:13). But, the author of the report himself admits two pages later, the excess of boys in the North is far greater than could be explained by mere omission. A recount was taken in the province of Ajmere, located in what is now Rajasthan, when the astounding report of twice as many males as females in the overall population was returned. The recount came up with the same figure. It was also shown that in Ajmere the proportion of children to adults was one of the lowest in all of British India, a situation that points clearly to infanticide (General Report 1875:15).

One last theory rests on inaccuracy of age reporting such that girls under the age of twelve would be reported as adults, thus shrinking the percentage of juvenile females. No explanation is given as to why such a pattern of age misrepresentation might characterize the Northwest; it simply does not seem to make cultural sense. In fact, as is discussed in Appendix A, a pattern opposite to this seems much more likely—that girls in their later teens are reported as being *younger* than they actually are. If age misreporting were really the case, one would expect a correspondingly high number of females in the subsequent age category, that of 13–20 years. However, although there was found in the Northwest Provinces "a remarkable falling off in the number of girls between 10 and 13 years of age . . . ," there was found no corresponding increase in the 13–20 category (General Report 1875:14). Thus the reporting of juvenile females as adults could not be an explanation for high juvenile sex ratios.

These explanations are the major ones proposed in the 1872 Census. A most remarkable feature of the General Report is that female infanticide was not even mentioned as being a possible reason for sex ratio disparities among juveniles in northern India—remarkable especially since the issue was in the forefront of the minds of many British officials.

A Case Study

The area with the very highest juvenile sex ratios reported for any province in the 1872 Census is the Northwest Provinces located in the western plains portion of Uttar Pradesh. A juvenile sex ratio of 120.1 is certainly a significantly high sex ratio given its large juvenile population of 10,235,979. In this region the proportion of children under twelve is almost exactly one-third of the population, no greater than that in other areas. In a separate census volume on the Northwest Provinces, the proportions of juveniles are given in one-year intervals. I group these into two categories: those under ten and those under twelve (Table 3).[8]

Juvenile sex ratios in both age categories in each district in the Northwest Provinces are extremely high. Sex ratios of children under ten range from a low of 107.0 to a high of 121.8; in the under-twelve

8. Separate figures are provided in the census for Hindus, Muslims, and Christians. However, I largely examine only the Hindu majority. There are several indications that "the Muslim sex ratio" is not consistently higher than that of the Hindus, as some might expect; to the contrary Muslim sex ratios tend to be lower (see the case study presented here on Mainpuri District). Another reason for my neglect of Muslims as a separate population for analysis is the lack of ethnographic data for Muslims of the North and the South and upper and lower social classes upon which to develop even a crude model of "the culture of sex ratios" for them.

Table 3

Hindu males per 100 females under age 10 and under
age 12, Northwest Provinces, 1871

District	Males under 10 years	Males under 12 years
Moozuffernuggur	121.8	128.2
Meerut	119.6	126.2
Boolundshuhur	110.3	117.8
Allygurh	111.3	118 6
Bijnour	118.1	124 7
Moradabad	109.7	116 7
Budaun	111.4	120.0
Bareilly	109.0	115.5
Shajehanpore	107.0	114.1
Turrai	117.2	121.0
Muttra	115.4	122.2
Agra	112.4	119.0
Furruckabad	112.5	120.4
Mynpoory	120.3	129.7
Etawah	112.5	119.7
Etah	112.4	121.0
Jaloun	114.9	119.7

Source: India 1873. Vol. II:xxiv–xxv.

Note: The size of the population in each age category for each district is so large as to reduce the possibility of error in the sex ratios given to a minimum. All are over 100,000 persons with the following exceptions: the under-10 population of Turrai is 26,000 and its under-12 population is 35,074; Jaloun's under-10 population is 83,602.

category the range is from 114.1 to 129.7.[9] Mainpuri District, infamous for the practice of female infanticide, has among the highest sex ratios in both categories. In general, throughout the Northwest Provinces, there are about seven boys for every six girls. This in itself is somewhat alarming but when one considers that female infanticide was probably not practiced by all castes, then the proportions must be even more striking among the practicing groups. In order to estimate what such proportions might be, data from the district of Mainpuri are examined in detail.

9. The fact that in all cases sex ratios rise from the under-ten category to the under-twelve category is intriguing. It must indicate continuing neglect of females from infancy till the time of their marriage. Maternal mortality could not affect either of these categories since menarche, not to mention pregnancy, could only very rarely occur before the age of twelve years. Current average age of menarche in rural India is fourteen years (Indian Council of Medical Research 1972:172–173).

Table 4
Males per 100 females under age 10 and under age
12, by religious group, Mainpuri District, 1871

Religious group	Males under 10 years	Males under 12 years
Total population	120.3	125.6
Hindus	121.0	126.4
Muslims	107.7	112.3

Source: India 1873. Vol. II:xxxvii.

At the time of the 1871 Census the total district population of Mainpuri was 765,783. The sex ratio of this overall population was 126.0—the highest of any district in the Northwest Provinces and probably the highest in all of British India. Table 4 provides juvenile sex ratios for the total population of the district, and for the Hindu and Muslims.

The most obvious point to be gleaned from these data is that juvenile sex ratios of Hindus, in both age categories, are much higher than those of Muslims. Further, since Muslims constitute roughly 5 percent of the district population, it is Hindu sex ratios that have the preponderant influence on aggregate juvenile sex ratios for the district. Within the many Hindu groups of Mainpuri District, however, some are more often associated with female infanticide than others.

Most often cited as culprits are Rajputs, while Ahirs, who tend to imitate Rajputs, are almost as frequently mentioned (Neave 1910:88–89). Just these two caste groups constitute a fairly significant minority in the population: Ahirs are about 18 percent of the total population, Rajputs about 7 percent.[10] So roughly 25 percent of the population is charged with the practice of infanticide. Within these large caste categories it is noted that the Phatak division of the Ahir caste, which is 83 percent of that caste, is the worst offending group of Ahirs, as is the Chauhan clan of Rajputs. Chauhan Rajputs constitute 33 percent of all Rajputs in Mainpuri District.

The question may then be posed as to the frequency with which the various subgroups committed female infanticide. Did they kill all

10. Neave (1910) reports that Rajputs are 9 percent of the Mainpuri population, and notes that their numbers had increased greatly since the last census. Therefore I roughly estimated that in the 1870s, Rajputs were 7 percent of the district population.

their daughters as certain Chauhan Rajput families are reputed to have done? Or did some Ahirs and Rajputs preserve some, or even all, of their daughters? No doubt there were many variations in the degree of female preservation within families. Some of these will be taken into account below.

First assume that within 25 percent of the population each family allows one daughter to live and also has two sons. (Since some families probably preserved more daughters, while not all families, no matter how many children were born, would produce even one daughter and also two sons, this is a fairly extreme assumption.) Let us also assume that families of the remaining 75 percent of the population have children of even sex distribution, also probably an inaccurate reflection of the true situation in that some families in this category may also have practiced infanticide.

In the case of the first assumption, the "juvenile" sex ratio for the Rajputs and Ahirs (25% of the population) is 200.0 and for others 100.0. For the total juvenile population of the district it is 118.0. This latter figure is somewhat lower than what actually prevailed in 1872: for the under-ten category the sex ratio was 120.3, while for the under-twelve category it was 125.6. The fairly extreme assumption that roughly one-fourth of the population murders half of their female offspring may in fact be an accurate model of the situation.

Let us similarly examine the more limited example of the Phatak Ahirs and the Chauhan Rajputs. Again, assume that families in these groups had one daughter for every two sons, while all other families had evenly balanced proportions of girls and boys. In this case, we find that the juvenile sex ratio for the Phatak Ahirs and Chauhan Rajputs (17–25% of the population) is 200.0, while for others it is 100.0. The ratio for the total juvenile population of the district is 112.2. This assumption yields a juvenile sex ratio considerably below those reported in the census. Either many Phataks and Chauhans are preserving not even one daughter or else other clans are also practicing female infanticide and neglect. The latter possibility seems the more plausible.

This brief excursion into the Northwest Provinces, and especially Mainpuri District, provides an indication of the frequency of the practice of female infanticide in one of the most infanticide-endemic areas. It can be said that one-fourth of the population of the North-west Provinces murdered one-half of their female offspring: this of course is a model that smooths the rough edges of reality for the sake of clarity and drama. But, no matter how the model is stretched, there is no escaping the fact that juvenile sex ratios were extremely high in India's Northwest and that, therefore, female infanticide was not practiced by only a negligible number of families. To the contrary, female infanticide and fatal neglect were quite common there.

Other Censuses

A review of other decennial censuses reveals that neither the pattern of imbalances in the sex ratios nor the explanations proposed for them changes very little through the years. The possibility of underenumeration of females is still proposed. Indeed, a certain Dr. Cornish, the author of the Madras Report, suggested the following:

> The truth is that the great bulk of enumerations have been singularly obtuse in comprehending the fact that the counting of females was a matter of any importance in census work . . . in districts where the Census work was well done it will be found that the female population is invariably in excess of the male; in fact, the general accuracy of the results of any district may be judged by the way in which the proportions of the sexes have been recorded. [India 1881. Report. Vol. 1:54]

Thus the clever Dr. Cornish, comfortably situated in the South where the proportions of the sexes were "accurately" equal, could take potshots at his squirming northern counterparts who consistently came up with counts showing great excesses of males—counts that were, then, according to Cornish's index of accuracy very faulty indeed.

The 1881 Census Commissioner repeatedly mentions the conceal-ment of females in the Northwest Provinces and the Punjab as the reason behind the sex disparities there. At one point, though, he does devote a few lines to the subject of female infanticide, noting the possibility that it might have a slight effect in altering the sex ratio:

> We have also to consider the defect in the number of the sex occa-sioned by the practice of female infanticide. Though that practice, we may assume, has not had any serious effect on the proportions of the

sexes throughout, yet it is unquestionable that it has had an effect which is perceptible. It was stated, when the measures for the repression of infanticide were first introduced in the Northern Provinces, that out of over twelve thousand girls of one year alive, at least half were due to the preventive arrangements which had been brought into practice by the introduction of anti-infanticide measures. [India 1881. Report. Vol. I:60]

Infanticide is once again rejected as even a partial explanation for the sex imbalances in the North in the 1891 General Report (summarized in Natarajan 1971) where the author proposes another explanation:

The practice of premature cohabitation is more or less local, or restricted to certain castes . . . but none the less is this period a critical one for girls in India, if only on the ground of demand on the nervous system, for we find that irrespective of the second and later part of the conjugal arrangement in that country, out of the 13 million or so girls between 10 and 15 years of age, 49 per cent are married *in the Indian acceptation of that term.* [Natarajan 1971:31; emphasis mine]

This explanation has severely limited application. First, marriages were rarely consummated before the bride reached physical maturity, which is usually around the age of fourteen. Very few brides could become pregnant before the age of fourteen and thus be subject to maternal mortality. True, these years are psychologically taxing ones for girls; there may be suicides and other psychologically induced deaths for females. But this is by no means the only period in the life span when females die in greater numbers than males. In fact, data in the 1901 Census (India 1901:116) show that the decline in the proportion of girls is most marked from birth to the age of ten and the process is actually reversed *after* the age of ten!

My review of the censuses ends with the 1901 Census and the turn of the century. This census contains the most complete chapter on the sexual composition of the Indian population. There is an organized exposition of the variation of sex ratios by province, including allusions to variation by social status. We find, for instance, the following: "In the whole of Northern India females are more numerous amongst the lowest classes, who are also the poorest, than amongst those at the top of the social structure, and in Bengal, the tract where women are fewest is also the tract where the people are most prosperous" (India 1903:114). While in the South, in Madras Presidency, "there is no special tendency for the proportion of females to vary according to the social status of a caste, but it is unusually small in the case of the Malàyalam-speaking Bràhmans, the majority of whom allow only the oldest son of each family to marry within the caste, and leave the others to contract alliances with Nayar women" (India 1901:114). In spite of such analytical advancements, there is once again a reversion to the explanation of preponderance of males at birth, which occurs in the Northwest according to the census findings. Important among "other explanations" is the neglect of females which is acknowledged as replacing outright infanticide said to be "perhaps somewhat rare":

> Even if there is no deliberate design of hastening a girl's death, there is no doubt that, as a rule, she receives less attention than would be bestowed upon a son. She is less warmly clad, and less carefully rubbed with mustard oil as a prophylactic against the colds and chills to which the greater part of the mortality amongst children in India is due; she is probably not so well fed as a boy would be, and when ill, her parents are not likely to make the same strenuous efforts to ensure her recovery. . . . [India 1903:116]

But, given the inaccuracy of death reporting, it is hard to say just how much female mortality occurs at which ages. If for every one hundred surviving boys in the Northwest Provinces, ten fewer girls survive, then that is a rather large loss. However, in Mainpuri District, for every one hundred boys there were lost *seventeen* girls.

Although many believe that today outright female infanticide no longer exists in India, there is some evidence to the contrary. An Indian anthropologist, Majumdar, reports the following somber story:

> Although it is an offense punishable by death under the provisions of the Indian penal code, it is impossible to resist the conclusion that female children are even today made away with immediately after birth. . . . A high caste Association at its annual session about eight years back unequivocally condemned female infanticide among them, a voluntary admission which may be accepted as a token of their earnest desire to put an end to such cruel practices. [1947:222]

The condemnation of female infanticide by a caste association may also be taken as a voluntary admission that outright female infanticide was still practiced in the mid-twentieth century and may not be completely abandoned even now.

4
Variations in Indian
Sex Ratios Today

While imbalances in Indian sex ratios have been a subject of interest to scholars for many years, it is only recently that systematic analyses of the problem have been made. The most prominent of these are a study entitled *The Sex Ratio of the Indian Population* (Visaria 1961) and a dissertation, "Some Socio-Cultural Correlates of Indian Sex Ratios: Studies from Punjab and Kerala" (Kelly 1975).

Using data from Indian censuses, Visaria (1961) analyzes existing theories seeking to explain sex ratio imbalances in India. The most important of these concern migration, underenumeration of females, and sex ratio at birth. He refutes the validity of all of these as important factors. First, migration may be partially responsible for regional variations in the sex ratio but the excess of males in the northern part of India "is not primarily or mainly a result of sex-selective mobility to those areas" (1961:12). Visaria also denies that the underenumeration of females is an important factor, although he admits there is some evidence of slight underenumeration (1961:24). Strong support for the rejection of underenumeration as explanatory comes from the findings of the Khanna study, a project carried out for over a decade in eleven villages of the Punjab by a team of Harvard researchers and Indian collaborators (Wyon and Gordon 1971). The study involved careful and frequent census-taking in all the project villages. Khanna study findings confirm that females are not undercounted; they are simply not alive to be counted. Another independent source confirming Indian census data comes from data on sex ratios of Indians in Fiji, Mauritius, South Africa, and Singapore which again show a scarcity of females (Visaria 1961:48–49). The third possible explanation, that of sex ratio at birth, is also neatly dispatched by Visaria (1961:25–37). Scholars have devoted much time and effort to constructing theories about why sex ratios at birth vary (blood type, race, age of parents, climate). But as Visaria demonstrates, variations in sex ratio at birth throughout the subcontinent are actually minor and cannot be used as an explanation for the wide imbalances found in the population (see Appendix A).

Having rejected all of these theories, Visaria then considers the possibility of differentials in the mortality rates of males and females. This is the only explanation that the highly critical and careful author accepts (1961:38–47). After examining census data on mortality, which he admits are faulty, and supporting evidence from the northern Khanna study and a southern study from Ramnagaram (Karnataka), Visaria concludes that:

> Evidence on excess female mortality is indeed impressive. The magnitude of such female disadvantage in chances of survival seems to be large enough to explain a major part and sometimes the entire excess of males in the population of the North-Western areas of the subcontinent. There is suggestive indication of regional differences in sex ratios of population being associated with differences in the sex-pattern of mortality. Additional evidence will probably accumulate over time. [1961:47]

He considers that both higher mortality among girls, perhaps due to their mistreatment, and maternal mortality of women are major factors in higher female than male mortality. Kelly's study (1975) focuses on the former of these.

Kelly feels that the attribution of sex ratio differentials to mortality patterns fails to explain "how or why female mortality persists in certain regions even though general levels of mortality have declined significantly in the same areas" (1975:7). Her hypothesis is as follows:

> Female mortality is higher than male at ages other than childbearing in the Punjab and not in Kerala because Punjabi social structure and social practice puts [sic] a higher premium on male infant survival to

the detriment of the female. The large sex differentials in infant and childhood mortality found in the Northern states are responsible for their very high sex ratios. [1975:7]

Employing largely unpublished data from two studies, one done in the Punjab and the other in Kerala, Kelly does an admirable job of demonstrating that survival rates of daughters in the Punjab are lower than they are in Kerala (1975:132–135). She also makes a strong case for differentials in the treatment of girls and boys, especially in the allocation of medical care, as the immediate cause of impaired survival of girls in the Punjab (1975:135–136).

Besides Visaria and Kelly there are no major analytic works of high quality on Indian sex ratios, though several other articles and books exist on specific aspects of the subject. Some of these take a historical perspective (Desai 1967; Visaria 1967a; Dutta 1961). Others are aimed at a specific regional or social segment of the Indian population (Dange 1972; Pakrasi 1964; Siddiqui 1976; Sidhu and Anand 1972). Some seek to argue specific reasons for sex ratio imbalances, like race (Basu 1963) or nutrition (Gopalan and Naidu 1972); still others focus on the urban situation. Most studies that deal with variations in the Indian sex ratio have focused exclusively on regional patterns, ignoring possible social differences (Gosal 1961; Reith 1975). Dange's article on sex ratios in Madhya Pradesh is an exception for it alludes to different sex ratio patterns between tribals and nontribals in that state (1972). He finds that while the sex ratios of nontribal people vary by region with more males relative to females in the wheat areas to the west than in the rice areas to the east, there is "a relative deficiency of males over females among the scheduled tribes, irrespective of crop-regions" (1972:282). Speaking against the hypothesis that there are differences in sex ratios according to social structure, Kelly notes that, while in the past there were more males than females in higher status groups of the Punjab, today "higher female mortality early in life is not a function of socio-economic status groups" (Kelly 1975:17). It is my hypothesis that sex ratios must vary according to socioeconomic class because the cultural framework in which sex ratio patterns are embedded also varies by class.

Regional variation in Indian sex ratios is a well-accepted fact;

social variation is not. The present task concerning regional variation will involve only a refinement of work that has been done so far on that subject. Refinement involves bringing the level of analysis from the state level, where it has usually been performed, to the district level.[1] In this way we move from a consideration of 19 observations to 323. Patterns that have already been shown to exist at the state level are more clearly portrayed. Consideration of the age delineation of the population adds another degree of refinement. Usually only the overall population is discussed, but this study focuses on the juvenile population (under the age of ten years). In this way effects of female infanticide and fatal neglect can be most easily seen without the distortions of factors, such as migration and maternal mortality, which affect the balance of the sexes among adults. To analyze social variation in sex ratios, I use census data on several castes from the North and the South. The examination of sex ratios by caste adds an entirely new dimension to previous studies, and it is my hope that future researchers will be inspired to tackle this area.

Regional Variation

According to the 1961 Census of India (vol. I, pt. 1:307) the sex ratio for India as a whole is 1,063 males per 1,000 females. This figure itself is neither surprising nor perplexing. It is quite similar to overall sex ratios for most of the countries of the Middle East and for Pakistan while it is slightly higher than the more equal sex ratios of Southeast Asia (Desai 1969:5; El-Badry 1969:1235). The overall Indian sex ratio of 1,063 conceals regional variations that are more interesting. Generally speaking, the northwestern states have high sex ratios. The state of Punjab has the highest of any state, 1,157 (Visaria 1961:3). Sex ratios in the southern and eastern states are much lower. Kerala has the lowest sex ratio of any state, 979. Yet these figures for the

1. To display regional variation in juvenile sex ratios, I have employed 1961 Census of India figures, as the 1971 Census is still not entirely complete. For the study of social patterns, my source is data by caste from the 1931 Census of India. This census contains the most recent data on caste as later censuses refrained from employing the category as a result of the abolishment in 1948 of discrimination on the basis of caste by the independent Indian government. The 1941 Census contains data on caste but the census is incomplete because of wartime conditions.

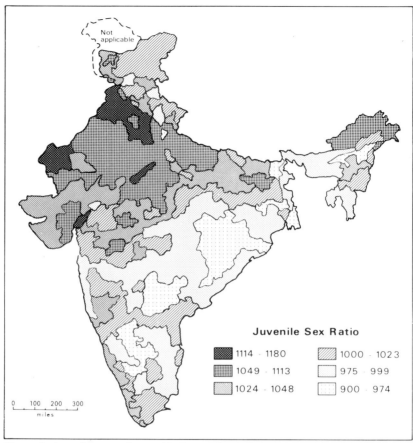

Figure 4 Juvenile sex ratio, rural India, 1961. Juveniles are children under 10 years of age; sex ratio refers to the number of males per 1,000 females.

overall population cloak an even more striking contrast between the North and the South which becomes apparent when sex ratios for juveniles are determined and mapped by district (Fig. 4).[2]

In looking at the district-level pattern of juvenile sex ratios in rural India, one is struck by this remarkably clear pattern of deficit of females in a large area in the Northwest. The range of juvenile sex

2. Sopher (1980:297) provides a similar map, though the data are broken down into fifths, not sixths as here.

ratios extends from a high of 1,180 males (per 1,000 females) in Rajas-than's Jaisalmer District, to a low in Orissa's Koraput District. Thirty percent of all India's rural districts have juvenile sex ratios over 1,049, which is above what can be considered "normal" for popula-tions in the tens of thousands. This group of "suspicious" districts forms almost a solid triangular area stretching from Gujarat to Bihar, a distribution very similar to that found in Figure 3. (The high sex ratio in the Northeastern Frontier Agency should be viewed with caution as the population is sparse and the census count of 1961 is in doubt there.) Except for a few districts in Madhya Pradesh, none of the "suspicious" districts is found south of the Vindhya-Narmada divide and thus this pattern closely conforms to the North-South model dichotomy, a dichotomy worth discussing in greater detail.

The two regions, the North and the South, have a long-standing history of distinctness. History provides a picture of Aryan penetra-tions from Central Asia through the mountain passes of the North-west, beginning around 2500 B.C. It is generally believed that these incursions displaced and partly absorbed the indigenous population, but with diminished impact in the East, South, and north to the Himalayan zone. The Narmada River, which crosses through the western part of the subcontinent, served as a barrier keeping the Aryans and their culture from spreading further into the southern part of the peninsula. The mere factor of distance probably contributed to the slowness with which the Aryans and their Vedic ways penetrated the East. Thus the stronghold of the Aryans is the Northwest, while that of the earlier population is South and East where Dravidian languages survive; Brahmanical culture is strongest in the Northwest; Dravidian or Agamic culture is most prominent in the South and East.[3]

Hinduism is more widespread throughout the population in the North, a fact which is reflected in the higher percentage of Brahmans in the population of the North than elsewhere (Sopher 1980:167). There is also a rough correspondence with agricultural practices:

3. To avoid the possibly racist overtones of the terms Aryan and Dravidian, which are neither entirely relevant nor entirely accurate, I have used the terms Brahmanic and Agamic, respectively, instead. These latter terms are derived from ancient religious and literary traditions.

dry-field plough cultivation characterizes the northern plain while wet rice cultivation is common in the South and East, and land tenure patterns show much higher percentages of landlessness in the South than in the North (Schwartzberg 1961). Cultural differences between the North and South are discussed in detail in subsequent chapters.

Social Variation

The study of social variation in sex ratios is not easily undertaken. The modern censuses of India do not provide sex ratios according to any sophisticated class categorization. Nor do censuses after the 1931 Census of India give sex ratios for different caste groups. Given the choice between using modern data for just three categories (Scheduled Tribes, Scheduled Castes, and the non-Scheduled population) or using somewhat old data on castes, I opted for the latter. This method provides for a degree of continuity between the examination of sex ratios in the twentieth century and the review of social variation in the practice of female infanticide in the nineteenth century. Further, it is possible very roughly to translate castes into classes.

Such a translation is possible because *generally* upper castes are predominantly composed of people in the upper class, which I define simply as being "propertied." Similarly, lower castes are primarily composed of people who are "unpropertied" and thus of the lower class. Most anthropologists with experience in India could rank the more populous castes of India into upper or lower categories; thus everyone would agree that Brahmans are *generally* upper caste, while Chamars are not. My simple system would then translate Brahmans into upper class and Chamars into lower class. The assignment here of any caste to a certain class rests, of course, with me, and is based on my reading of the ethnographic literature on rural India. Support for this procedure comes from statements by many ethnographers to the effect that, in the villages where they studied, the caste hierarchy is generally parallel with the class structure in spite of aberrant cases (Beck 1972:2; Djurfeldt and Lindberg 1975:216; Sivertsen 1963:56; Béteille 1962; Miller 1975:160; Lewis 1965:81; Freed and Freed 1976:111).

A serious terminological problem arises in the use of the word "caste." Recently this term has been almost completely dropped from the anthropological vocabulary in favor of *jāti*. Jati refers to an endogamous group, generally commensal, and sometimes associated with a particular occupation. Varna is an abstract term referring to large clusters of jatis. Generally there are believed to be four varnas: Brahman (priest), Kshatriya (warrior), Vaishya (merchant), and Shudra (worker). Neither of these terms fits the groups that I wish to discuss here, groups that are somewhere in between jati and varna. Therefore I am resurrecting the term "caste" to fit the pre-independence use of that term for clusters of jatis, but smaller clusters than are included in a varna. I follow the 1931 Census of India's caste designations. Thus a Kanya Kubja Brahman of northern India belongs to the Kanya Kubja jati but would be returned as belonging to the Brahman caste. Likewise a Smartha Brahman of Madras and a Gaur Brahman of Delhi belong to entirely different jatis but to the same caste, according to census terminology.

My hypothesis here is that castes of the upper level, of which the majority of the members are propertied, will display juvenile sex ratio patterns characteristically different from those of the lower level. The bases for this view are, first, the apparent social variation in the practice of outright female infanticide in the nineteenth century which might be carried over into the twentieth-century practice of female neglect, and, second, the pressures on property-holding families to bear sons as heirs. The data, as we shall soon see, reflect on this hypothesis in a very interesting way.

I selected three well-known castes for each regional/class category: northern propertied, northern unpropertied, southern propertied, and southern unpropertied. The castes selected are found mainly in the United Provinces (present Uttar Pradesh) and Madras (which comprised parts of present-day Kerala, Andhra Pradesh, and Tamil Nadu).

The Jats, Rajputs, and Ahirs were chosen to represent the category of northern propertied (Fig. 5a). All three groups are found primarily in the western part of the state, though Rajputs and Ahirs spread further to the east. They all exhibit a clear pattern of female deficit in the early childhood years with some exceptionally high sex ratios in the 7–13 category. This cannot be explained by either marriage

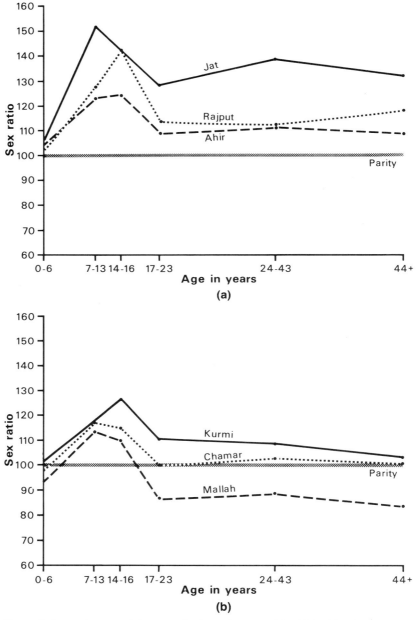

Figure 5 Sex ratios at certain ages of selected castes of the United Provinces, 1931: *a,* propertied castes (Jat, Rajput, Ahir); *b,* unpropertied castes (Kurmi, Chamar, Mallah). Sex ratio refers to males per 100 females.

migration or maternal mortality since neither of these occurs significantly before menarche, currently estimated on the all-India level at fourteen years of age (see Chapter 3, n. 9). Nor is there any reason to suppose that the sex ratio imbalances are a statistical chimera due to the small size of the population under consideration: these are very large caste groups. The Jat sex ratio is the most remarkable, peaking at 156 (males per 100 females) in the age bracket of 7–13, while the Rajput sex ratio here is 127, and the Ahir 123. In the next age category, 14–16, the proportion of male Jats drops to meet the rising sex ratio of the Rajputs at the still very high 142, while the Ahir ratio rises to 124.[4] Clearly, some of the "suspected" castes of 1881 still (in 1931) look very suspicious.

The pattern of the above groups, when compared with that of the unpropertied castes of the United Provinces, shows a certain degree of isomorphy, though the lower castes' juvenile sex ratios are much less masculine than those of the upper castes (Fig. 5b). Sex ratios examined here are of three generally landless and poor castes of the United Provinces: the Kurmi, the Chamar, and the Mallah. While Chamars and Mallahs are found throughout the province, Kurmis are found primarily in the eastern portion. Both the Chamar and Mallah sex ratios are highest at the 7–13 bracket, being 117 and 114 respectively. The Kurmi sex ratio is also 117 at this age but rises to its peak of 126 at the 14–16 age bracket, while the sex ratios of Chamars and Mallahs descend to 115 and 110. Thus while none of the upper castes has sex ratios descending from the 7–13 category to the 14–16 category, both Chamars and Mallahs do. Otherwise all castes display a similar amount of slope in the initial rise from 0–6 to 7–13, though there is great variation in the sex ratios reached at the later category.

Now look at the juvenile sex ratios of three propertied castes of Madras: the Vanniyan, the Telaga, and the Tamil Brahman (Fig. 6a). The striking feature here is that the highest sex ratio reached by any

---

4. The decline of masculinity seen in the 14–16 group continues for the most part in the move to the 17–23 bracket, and even accelerates. But it cannot be assumed that mortality is the major factor affecting sex ratios among adults as migration may come into play. However, the very clarity of this pattern for such large groups in both North and South points to some factor or factors other than migration as an explanation; this problem certainly constitutes an important avenue of research.

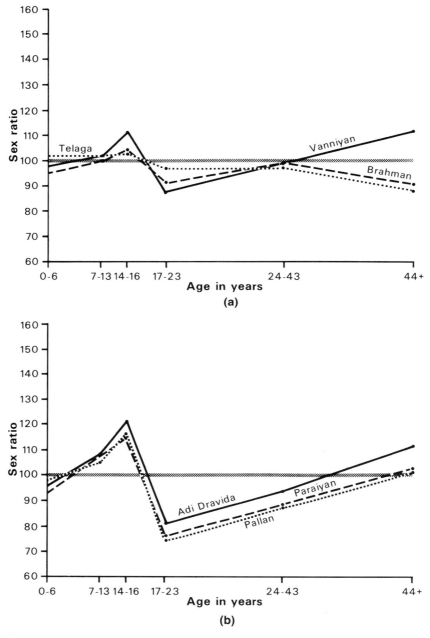

Figure 6 Sex ratios at certain ages of selected castes of Madras, 1931: *a*, propertied castes (Telaga, Vanniyan, Brahman); *b*, unpropertied castes (Adi Dravida, Pallan, Paraiyan). Sex ratio refers to males per 100 females.

of these castes is only 111 (at the 14–16 age bracket); this is lower than almost any youthful sex ratio of any northern caste previously examined. Only the Mallahs with a sex ratio of 110 in the 14–16 category have a sex ratio lower than the highest sex ratio among these southern propertied castes. This is remarkable. Another noteworthy point is that while all these southern castes exhibit a general rise from the 0–6 group through to the 14–16 group, the ascent is by no means steep compared with the northern pattern. The Vanniyan sex ratio goes from 97–102–111; the Telaga from 101–102–103; and the Tamil Brahman from 96–100–103. All of these sex ratios are within the general range of expectation except for the Vanniyan sex ratio of 111 in the 14–16 group which may be indicative of differential mortality. Another point of comparison with the northern pattern is that, while many of the northern castes reach their masculinity peak at the 7–13 age bracket, none of the southern castes do; the Telaga sex ratio changes only one point between 0–6 and 7–13; Tamil Brahman and Vanniyan sex ratios change about ten points and thus seem a bit more northern.

Sex ratios for landless laboring castes in the South exhibit a different, more extreme pattern of ascent followed by a large dip in the adult years (Fig. 6b). All start out with very feminine sex ratios in the 0–6 category, between 94 and 97. Then all rise to the 7–13 and 14–16 categories: the Adi-Dravida go from 96–107–121; the Para-iyan from 94–108–115; the Pallan from 97–105–116. The sex ratios of these castes in the 14–16 category are quite high, though not nearly as high as sex ratios of northern propertied groups. This pattern will become more understandable when a comparison of sex ratios of northern and southern high castes and then northern and southern low castes is made. First look at the Rajputs as compared with the Tamil Brahmans of the South. While the sex ratios of the southern Brahmans hover near the line of parity (100), those of the Rajputs never touch that line. The greatest distance between the two occurs at the age brackets 7–13, 14–16, and 17–23. A comparison of two "cultivating castes" (in which the peasants themselves work the fields) also shows great differences. Here sex ratios of the northern Jats are compared with those of the Telaga of Andhra Pradesh. Again the sex ratios of the southern caste hover around the parity line while those of the northern caste avoid the range of expectability except at the 0–6 age category. The last example takes two unpropertied castes: the northern Chamars and the Paraiyans of Madras. This is the only case in which the sex ratios of the two castes come close to, and even touch, each other. The two patterns are strikingly similar, each rising and descending in relation to the line of parity at roughly the same points.

From all these sex ratios—northern and southern, propertied and unpropertied—a generalization concerning the relationship between class and sex ratio can be made. There are three patterns of juvenile sex ratios according to socioeconomic status in India: (1) the northern propertied pattern which exhibits very high masculinity, (2) the southern propertied pattern which exhibits equality or female preponderance, and (3) the all-India unpropertied class pattern of masculine juvenile sex ratios. Thus the hypothesis that all propertied groups will have higher juvenile sex ratios than unpropertied groups has been amended: such applies only to the North.

Juvenile Mortality Statistics

If the hypothesis that differentials in mortality between boys and girls are the primary factor creating imbalances in juvenile sex ratios is correct, then female mortality should be particularly high in northern propertied groups. Regrettably, mortality statistics in Indian censuses are so inadequate as to be unusable here (Dandekar 1977:223). Intensive studies of mortality in localized areas can be consulted, though their representativeness is limited. The following is a review of some mortality statistics from two studies in the North and two studies in the South (Table 5): the Khanna study which took place in Ludhiana District, Punjab (Wyon and Gordon 1965, 1971); the Narangwal study also done in Ludhiana District (Kelly 1975); the Kottayam study carried out in Kottayam District, Kerala (Kelly 1975); and the Vellore project, an ongoing study in the area of Vellore city, Chingleput District (Sundar Rao 1978).

In the infant category the female mortality rate in both Punjab studies is much higher than the male mortality rate. In the Vellore study, female mortality is slightly *lower* than that for males, a situa-

Table 5
Juvenile mortality statistics from North and South India

	Sex differentials in infant (0–1 years) mortality rates[a]		
Sex	Khanna study (1957–59, 11 villages)	Narangwal study (1969–70, 22 villages)	Vellore study (2,167 deaths)
Male	114.6	125.0	120.4
Female	168.4	196.0	111.7
Total (both sexes)	156.2	148.0	116.2

	Sex differentials in childhood mortality rates[b]		
Sex	Khanna study	Narangwal study	Vellore study
Male	19.4	29.0	21.6
Female	36.9	58.0	25.1
Total (both sexes)	27.4	42.0	23.3

	Sex ratio at death during childhood[c]		
Age	Narangwal study	Vellore study	Kottayam study
under 1 month	126	92[d]	
1–5 months	114	134	
6–11 months	73	141	161[e]
1 year	62	109	
1–4 years	71	86	123[f]

Sources: Kelly 1975:132, Sundar Rao 1978, Wyon and Gordon 1971:186.
[a]Infant mortality rate in the Khanna and Narangwal studies refers to deaths per 1,000 births; in the Vellore study it refers to deaths per 1,000 population.
[b]Childhood mortality rate is deaths per 1,000 population per year, 1–4 years.
[c]Sex ratio refers to males per 100 females.
[d]Under 28 days.
[e]Under 1 year.
[f]Under 5 years.

tion more akin to what is found in Western countries for the first year of life. Childhood mortality rates also indicate different situations in the North and the South. In the Khanna and Narangwal study areas female mortality rates are almost twice as high as male mortality rates. In the Vellore study, only slightly higher rates for females were found.

Looking at mortality sex ratios for different childhood periods taken from the Narangwal study in the North and the two southern studies from Kottayam and Vellore, contrasts again appear pointing to higher death rates for girls (as compared with boys) in the North than in the South. Sex ratios at death are high—that is, deaths are

preponderantly male—in the Narangwal area only in the first five
months of life; thereafter female deaths are preponderant. There is
almost the opposite pattern portrayed by the southern studies where
sex ratios at death are often much higher for boys.

These studies make clear that there are different patterns of mortality for boys and girls in North and South India: girls die at much
higher rates than boys in the North while death rates are more equal in
the South. These statistics, gained through reliable studies of large
groups over long periods of time, confirm the hypothesis that unbalanced juvenile sex ratios in the North are indeed the result of sex
differentials in mortality.

5
Differentials in Child Care

Differences in mortality between boys and girls in North India are largely the immediate result of favoritism toward boys and the relative neglect of girls. Discrimination occurs mainly in three categories: feeding, dispensation of medical care, and allocation of love and warmth.

Food

No one would question that poor nutrition can result in death, for everyone is cognizant of the extreme state of poor nutrition—starvation. Yet between good health based on adequate nutrition and starvation unto death lies a broad spectrum of physical conditions dependent on varying degrees of poor-to-good nutrition which are matched by states of poor-to-good health.

This range of health can best be approached by looking at what medical scientists have determined to be the most vulnerable periods of life in terms of nutritional needs for each sex. These periods can be compared with those that are the most and the least culturally protected for each sex. As Greenough has shown in his work on the Bengal famine of 1943–1944 (1977, 1982), these two patterns—the biological and the cultural—often do not correspond. For instance, culture may dictate that adult men should be fed the best and most food, yet adult men might not have the nutritional needs of adolescent boys or girls.

The most dangerous periods in a person's life are thus the points at which the lack of cultural protection coincides with a biological period of great nutritional need. Universally, in the juvenile age group, the two most nutritionally demanding periods are infancy (0–1 years) and puberty (Jelliffe 1966; Whyte 1974:111–127). It is during these times that the human body is growing the fastest and needs the most protein and calories.

All cultures have priorities in the distribution of food. Such patterns are highly revealing of the valued members of that culture, yet little work has been done on this fascinating subject. Perhaps the slowly increasing interest of anthropologists in the cultural aspects of food and nutrition will help to correct the situation (Fitzgerald 1977).

Reports on nutrition and feeding practices in India are abundant, but for my purposes most are useless. Usually the data are not disaggregated by sex (Hasan 1971; Gokulanathan and Verghese 1969; Anand and Rama Rao 1962; Swaminathan 1976; May 1961; Rao et al. 1961; Ghosh 1966), or few specifics are given on male-female differences (Jyothi et al. 1963). Gross inaccuracies may indicate a cursory study at best (Akhtar 1971).[1] Kar (1968) provides a lengthy annotated bibliography of many nutrition studies on India which is quite helpful, and Whyte's *Rural Nutrition in Monsoon Asia* (1974) amasses data from a large number of findings on India but gives scant mention to sex differentials in nutrition and feeding practices.

Infancy. The discussion of discrimination in the allocation of food has an obvious beginning: breast feeding and weaning of infants. It has been hypothesized that a new mother needs to feel secure and happy in order to commence successful breast feeding of her infant (Raphael 1973).[2] Two features of North Indian culture could adversely affect the mother's feeling of security and thus her ability to nurse. These are, first, the common practice of giving birth (especially after the first child) in the home of the husband and, second, the strong desire for sons over daughters. The first of these deprives the mother of being

1. Wadley (1977), who worked in Karimpur where Akhtar did his survey, noted several errors of large magnitude in Akhtar's report.

2. There is no clinical data of which I am aware supporting this hypothesis; it seems, however, fairly plausible and certainly merits serious investigation.

surrounded by her natal kin with whom she feels more secure. The second—the desire for sons so intense that it can lead to great disappointment at the birth of a daughter—is undoubtedly aggravated when the birth takes place in the husband's home, for the husband's home is where the pressure to bear sons is the greatest on a young wife. Cultural elements surrounding the birth of a son in the North mark it as a joyous occasion; these are worth examining more closely because of the effect they could have on a new mother's unconscious feeling toward her infant.

Celebration at the birth of a son in the North, particularly a first son, has been documented repeatedly (Lewis 1965:49; Freed and Freed 1976:123, 206; Jacobson 1970:307–309; Madan 1965:63; Aggarwal 1971:114; Wadley 1975:42).[3] But when a daughter is born, the event is usually heralded by silence. Ethnographers have reported the unconcealed disappointment of families in which many girls are born (Luschinsky 1962:82; Madan 1965:77–78). Minturn and Hitchcock (1966:101–102) say that "the birth of a girl occasions no public ceremony. One informant, in fact, declared that when a girl is born, the mother hides, although this is an overstatement." Conversely, when a boy is born in the same Rajput community, a sweeper comes to beat a drum at the door of the happy household, Brahman women gather to sing joyous songs, a branch of a sacred tree is put over the doorway to the mother's room for good luck, and a yellow cord is placed around the boy's waist for protection.

It is noteworthy that despair at the birth of a girl is not a recurrent theme in ethnographies on village life in South India. There was even an explicit statement in one report that daughters are welcomed among the Udaiyar, the dominant caste in a non-Brahman village in Salem District, Tamil Nadu: "While the birth of sons is held to assure that the parents will be cared for in old age and their funeral rites properly carried out, the birth of a daughter is said to occasion delight" (Burkhart 1969:119). The only other reference I discovered in the literature on the South is from Dumont who says that among the Pramalai Kallar of Tamil Nadu, if the newborn is a boy "les femmes présentes poussent

3. Even where the birth is not announced formally until weeks or months later there is a naming ceremony that is more likely to be a "big affair" for a boy than for a girl (Leaf 1978).

onze *kulavei* ou cris roulés"[4] and one of them distributes sugar (1957*b*:236). In comparison to the northern pattern this is a very moderate expression of son preference indeed!

Thus while descriptions of joy at the birth of sons and celebrations of that joy are abundant in the northern village studies, there is no counterpart to be found in the literature on southern villages. Could it be that ethnographers in the South consistently missed such celebrations or simply failed to write about them? I doubt that the several anthropologists who wrote very careful studies of South Indian villages could all have been consistently less observant or less competent than anthropologists who studied northern villages. The more logical explanation is that there are few such marked differences in the announcement or celebration of the birth of a boy as compared with the birth of a girl in the South.

The question now arises whether it is possible that the quietness, sadness, and disappointment surrounding the birth of a girl, especially when that girl is born in the husband's home where the new mother lacks the warmth and support of her natal family, could sadden the mother so much that she unconsciously rejects the infant, fails to take it to her breast or to be able to feed it. I have no documentation of such an occurrence, although a somewhat parallel situation is reported by Wiser:[5]

> Balram's wife burst into our courtyard asking that someone come with her to see what was wrong with [her] . . . youngest daughter's new baby son. . . . The baby was three days old. . . . In a dark corner of the long storeroom, we found the young mother and her baby son who refused to take any nourishment. The mother lay on a sagging cot, in great pain. She said that she could not nurse him. Balram's wife took the baby in her arms to demonstrate the difficulty she had in trying to feed him. She dipped a small rag into a clay saucer of milk and put it into his mouth. He sucked a few times, and evidently getting very little, gave up. She put down the rag and said "There is nothing more that I can do. It is hopeless." He looked like a perfectly normal infant and I was troubled. . . . Two days later they told us that the baby had died. They were sorry, but what could they do, more than they had done? [1978:85]

4. This phrase translates as "the women present utter eleven *kulavei* or undulating cries."

5. My thanks to David Beatty, doctoral student in the Anthropology Department at Syracuse University, for pointing out this passage to me.

Wiser pondered this strange death and finally found an explanation for it from an old woman of the village:

> After the wedding, just nine months before, the bride had gone to the husband's home along with the wedding party. This is customary. But this initial visit is supposed to be brief, not more than three or four days. . . . [The bride] is carefully chaperoned and should only glimpse her husband when he comes into the courtyard for meals. While he is present, she sits in a corner and keeps her face discreetly covered. They are not supposed to speak to, or touch, one another. . . . After this visit, the bride returns home for some time. . . . In this instance, Balram, who was supposed to go for his daughter, neglected his duty. . . . The girl was left in her husband's home for at least a fortnight, during which time she became pregnant. In village eyes this was a disgrace, for which Balram, as her father, was to blame. . . . Had the child lived, neither the baby nor his mother would have been popular. In every society there are unwanted babies and this was one of them. [1978:86]

The explanation given to Wiser makes it clear that the baby was not wanted and thus conveniently "died." The failure of the young mother to be able to nurse the baby could have been rooted in shame at having become pregnant "illegitimately" (according to cultural rules) or perhaps the child was never even put to the breast. We don't know. What this sad example does tell us, though, is that if a child is not "right" there are ways that its life can be terminated. Just as the "illegitimate" child in the Wiser story was not considered "right" by the villagers, so also a girl child might be not considered "right" and treated in a like manner.

Leaving behind the provocative possibility of cultural blocks to the acceptance and feeding of a newborn, let us proceed to the period of weaning, a time that has been proved to be of great danger to infant survival. Scrimshaw, Taylor, and Gordon examine data from eleven Punjabi villages and four Guatemalan villages and find that the weaning period in both areas is highly correlated with the weanling diarrhea rate (1968:240–241). The relationship between weanling diarrhea mortality and nutrition is explained by the authors:

> Although the introduction of contaminated foods explains the increase in diarrheal episodes in the weaning and post-weaning periods, it does not, in itself, account for high mortality. Even given the factor of a higher dosage of infectious agents, experience elsewhere indicates that

such high death rates from diarrheal diseases are not seen in populations of well-nourished children. The answer seemingly is in an existing synergism between nutrition and infection. As malnutrition develops because of the poor weaning diet, acute diarrheal disease becomes increasingly likely to lead to death. At the same time, diarrheal disease reduces appetite, increases metabolic loss of nitrogen, and leads to further dietary restriction, all of which hastens the lowering of resistance to infection. [1968:253]

These early views have been reinforced by other more recent work on the relationship between poor nutrition, mortality, and weaning diarrhea (Behar 1975; Harries 1976; Mata et al. 1976; Newell et al. 1976; Rohde and Northrup 1976). Rohde and Northrup (1976:339) state that "with attack rates exceeding two episodes per year in the young, diarrhea with attendant dehydration is by far the major single killer in the developing world."

Two important studies, both done in the Punjab, demonstrate that weanling diarrhea does not strike the sexes equally—I refer to the Khanna and the Morinda studies. Of the major causes of death of infants in the Khanna study area reported by Gordon, Singh, and Wyon (1965), infantile diarrhea diseases were much more widespread among infant girls. The greater presence of the disease among girls was paralleled by higher death rates for girls:

> Death rates in the first year of life were 168.4 per 1,000 live births for females and 144.6 for males. . . . A much sharper distinction between death rates for males and females was evident in the second year of life, when the rates were respectively, 45.7 per 1,000 population of that age and 103.8 or more than twice as great. Acute diarrheal disease, the leading cause of death, was responsible for seven deaths of males and 18 of females. [1965:911–912]

The Morinda study was undertaken by Levinson (1972) in order to analyze the "determinants" of malnutrition in Punjabi children. He studied seventeen villages with a total population of about 13,000 people within a five-mile radius of Morinda town, Ropar District. Having considered many variables that might affect the nutritional status of children aged 6–24 months (economic status, beliefs of the mother, literacy of the mother) he concludes that:

> the most statistically significant determinant of nutritional status is sex. In other words, a child's sex per se would more consistently account for

variations in nutritional status than any of the other variables. Similarly, sex has emerged as a determinant, although less statistically significant of caloric intake for the population as a whole, and of diarrheal infection among Jats. [1972:72]

This conclusion contrasts with the finding of Jelliffe that in West Bengal, poverty is the main etiologic factor affecting children's nutritional status: ". . . in almost all cases poverty or economic inability to purchase costly protein foods, such as animal milk, was the prime etiologic factor, often associated with repeated attacks of enteritis and intestinal parasitism" (Jelliffe 1957:130).[6]

It is interesting that the sex differential in diarrheal infection is significant among the upper-class Jats of Levinson's study while it is not among the lower-class Ramdasias. Levinson attempts to explain this lack of sex disparity by assuming that among the Ramdasia only the most fit girls survive, the others are dead:

> Ramdasia females actually have slightly less major disease and diarrheal infection than Ramdasia males. In fact, it is likely that the malnourished Ramdasia female stricken with a major disease or with severe diarrheal infection simply does not survive. This contention would be supported by the much higher infant mortality rates for females (196 per 1,000) than for males (125 per 1,000) found by the Narangwal RHRC. . . . Among low income families these differences would be even more pronounced. Thus a Ramdasia female child who remains in the sample would likely have somewhat less frequent and severe diarrheal infection, although more than her Jat counterpart, and probably would not have had more than one major disease. [1972:76][7]

Levinson's reasoning here is faulty. In the first place, citing Narangwal mortality figures does not clarify the situation, as these figures are not broken down into upper- and lower-class rates for male and female children; in other words, figures showing that *female* infant mortality rates are higher than *male* infant mortality rates do not support his contention that *Ramdasia* female mortality rates are higher than those of *Ramdasia* male infants; the figures are unrelated to this problem. Furthermore he cannot automatically assume, with no

6. This finding may not apply to the entire population as most of the patients at the clinic where Jelliffe worked were from low-income families.

7. The Narangwal RHRC refers to the Rural Health Research Centre at Narangwal in Ludhiana District, Punjab.

data of his own on sex differentials of mortality by class, that "among low income families these differences would be even more pronounced." This is an unsupported and biased conjecture; the author is prone to think that whatever problems exist in the upper class also exist in the lower class though to an even greater degree since the lower class is poor and illiterate. In this way Levinson fights his data which I feel show that female Ramdasia children do not compare as poorly with male Ramdasia children as Jat girls do with Jat boys.

In an excellent review of infant feeding practices in many countries, Jelliffe (1968) discusses some differences that have been reported in the duration of breast feeding for boys and girls. Jelliffe first makes the generalization that in Moslem countries girls are often breast-fed for a slightly longer period than boys, perhaps since they are believed to be weaker (1968:32–84). A study in the Sudan, which Jelliffe reports (1968:38), found that boys are weaned between the ages of 18–24 months, while girls, "being only half men," continue to be breast-fed until they are between 24–30 months old. In Iran (Ghadimi 1957:625) girls are nursed for about 24 months while boys are nursed only until they are 22 months old. In Lebanon it was found (Patai 1965:269, quoted in Prothro 1967:74) that boys are nursed longer than girls, both in villages in Beqaa valley and in the city of Beirut. It is noteworthy that all these reports come from the Middle East. Jelliffe does not mention reports of different weaning times for boys and girls in Africa, the Far East, or the Western hemisphere, though such undoubtedly do exist.

How does the time of weaning affect the survival of the infant? The best generalization that can be made is that weaning either "too early" or "too late" can be very hazardous to the health of the child. Existing studies unfortunately make it impossible to define narrowly what is meant by "too early" or "too late" weaning. Generally, 6 months of age might be considered early, two years or more, late. Mata et al. (1976) distinguish between "early" and "late" infantile diarrhea, corresponding to early and late weaning. While both can be very serious and fatal, early diarrhea tends to be more dangerous: "In early diarrhoea the probability of severe malnutrition and premature death and other sequelae is greater than when weaning is late"

(1976:312). Delay in the giving of solid food is also associated with increased chances of death (Wyon and Gordon 1971:187). This is especially true after the age of 6 months when the quality of breast milk begins to decline. Still, the complete cessation of breast feeding in favor of solid foods before the age of 18 months is also very dangerous: "Between the ages of 12 and 18 months the few children taking solid food but no longer receiving breast milk had a higher death rate than children receiving breast milk and food. This suggests the importance of high quality protein as part of the diet of these ages" (Wyon and Gordon 1971:189). Confronted by the complex variables involved here—time of weaning, time of introduction of solids, quality and quantity of supplemental foods, time of complete cessation of breast feeding—what can we say about the situation in rural India?

Scattered reports of duration of breast feeding in India do indicate some preference for longer feeding for boys; two sources on the Punjab attest to this (Levinson 1976:75; Kelly 1975:140). Others note no sexual differences, that nursing lasts for two years on the average or until a subsequent pregnancy occurs (Beals 1974:9; Lewis 1965:49; Freed and Freed 1976:73; Jelliffe 1957:130; Rao and Bala-subramanian 1966:354). Lewis adds the detail that "if the youngest child was a boy, weaning might not occur until four years of age." Here we have a hint of something very important: if a child is nursed until the next one comes, then the sooner the next one comes is probably the worse for the child still nursing (1965:73). And, indeed, studies have shown that the interval between births is shorter after the birth of a girl than after the birth of a boy. Haldar and Bhattacharyya (1969) demonstrate this point using highly aggregate National Sample Survey data, and Khan (1973) comes to the same conclusion in his analysis of data from Patna town in Bihar. However, the difference is often only that of a few months.

Another clue to difference in weaning time between boys and girls in the North is reported by Luschinsky (1962:153). In discussing the performance of the Brahmanical sacrament of annaprāśana, or the ritual first feeding of solid foods to a child, the author notes that in Senapur (near Benares) this sacrament is often performed months earlier for a girl than for a boy, in spite of the fact that such variation is not sanctioned by classical texts on the performance of the Hindu sacraments (Pandey 1961:90–93).[8] While such sacramental weaning does not mean that the child no longer receives any breast milk, there is probably a lessening in the frequency of feeding. In stark contrast to the situation described by Luschinsky stands Jelliffe's (1957:130) description of the ceremony of *mukhe bhāt* ("rice eating," the modern equivalent of the Sanskritic rite of annaprasana). In West Bengal this is performed at the age of six months for a boy and seven months for a girl! Once again, no clear relationship can be drawn between the timing of the ritual and survival of the child as the amount of breast milk and solids is not known. Nevertheless, if nursing a child can be taken as a sign of caring, then such variations in timing are important.

Childhood and adolescence. From ethnographies of Indian villages, a general impression can often be gained of discrimination against girls in terms of food, but it is only an impression after all, since detailed information on actual consumption in terms of calories and proteins by sex and age is almost nonexistent in the anthropological literature. Wiser's study (1936) of food in Karimpur, Uttar Pradesh, is full of information on types of food consumed and how they are cooked, and contains some clues as to possible sex differentials in eating, but very little is reported on caste variations, or the differences in men's and women's diets. Planalp (1971) gathers together much important data on foods considered best for men and women and the consumption of calories by men and women and he also discusses unequal distribution of food within the family. The most complete anthropological study of differential nutrition within the family comes from Montgomery's (1972) work on nutrition and social stratification in a Tamil village, which exemplifies the kind of work greatly needed.

Nutritional status studies and ethnographic reports that indicate inferior feeding and nutrition of girls as compared with boys were compiled (Table 6). It is noteworthy that all villages and groups in

8. The only textually sanctioned sexual difference is that boys should be weaned during the even (auspicious) months of the year while girls should be weaned during odd (inauspicious) months.

Table 6

Allocation of food, medical care, and love to children, by research site

Index no.[a]	Research site and source	Food	Medical care	Love
1	Utrassu-Umanagri (Madan, 1965:78)	Elders believe that "overfeeding" girls makes them unattractive but hold no such concern about boys' overeating.		Sons receive more verbal expressions of love and are disciplined at a later age.
2	Goshen (Newell 1978)	Girls rather than boys often get special snacks.		Elders spend equal time caring for both sexes but boys receive more love, the youngest boy gets more affection.
A	Daleke, Amritsar District (Singh 1971:499)	Similar food is given to males and females, although boys who are in school may be given larger portions of butter and ghee.		
3	Shahidpur (Leaf 1978)	No sex differences.	Boys are given more expensive medical care than girls.	No sex differences.
B	Area around Chandigarh (Clements 1977)	Ghee and other luxury foods are given to boys.		
7	Shanti Nagar (Freed and Freed 1976:73)			Love and attention is generally lavished on child until next arrives.
8	Chavandi Kalan (Aggarwal 1978)	Girls are discriminated against in feeding but food is meager for all.	Boys are favored.	Boys receive slightly more love than girls; first son is usually spoiled.

Table 6—continued

Index no.[a]	Research site and source	Food	Medical care	Love
9	Khalapur (Minturn and Hitchcock 1966:77–78, 97)		Lack of concern is shown for health of girls; all four sick children receiving no medical care in neighborhood were girls.	When asked whether they would rather have a girl or boy, most elders say no preference; most say they *like* girls better.
11	Bunkipur (Marshall 1978)	Belief exists that students need "brain food" (milk, ghee); boys rather than girls tend to be students so they get more of limited good food.	Girls do not get equal medical care; higher, educated jatis are more equitable.	Infant boys, especially first sons, seem to get more attention.
12	Karimpur (Wadley and Derr 1978)	Boys are favored in terms of extras (snacks, sweets).	Girls get less and later care; rich families take better care of girls.	First children are cherished by mother and grandmother regardless of sex; mother cherishes first daughter even if others do not; a first son born after many daughters is especially loved.
14	Sherupur (Gould 1959: 53, 150)	Daughters who survive infancy are at most only slightly less well fed than boys, but a daughter ". . . is more readily expendable than a son."	Slight favoritism toward boys exists.	Daughters who survive infancy are only slightly less well cared for than sons.
15a	Senapur (Luschinsky 1962:181, 186)	Grandmother quoted as saying that if there is ghee, she gives it to the boys.	Elders spend money more freely for medical care of boys than of girls.	

15b	Madhopur (Planalp 1971:127)	Many women give scarce protein-rich food to men and children, especially sons.	No sex differences.
20	Rajpur (Poffenberger 1975:91)	Sons are fed first and given larger quantities than daughters.	Sons are believed to need special medical care ("a girl is like a stone and nothing can hurt her but a boy is like a flower and must be treated with care").
C_1	Six villages, Dhar District (Grewal, Gopaldas, and Gadre 1973:267)	Consistently higher percentage of girls than boys is malnourished.	
C_2	Six villages, Sehore District (Grewal, Gopaldas, and Gadre 1973:267)	Consistently higher percentage of girls than boys is malnourished.	
23	Nimkhera (Jacobson 1970:315)	No sex differences.	No sex differences.
39	Namhalli (Beals 1974:100)		Girls and later-born boys rarely receive medical care.
D	Tiruvanmiyar, Chingleput District (Cantor/Atac 1972:40–41)[b]	Girls are given special food during first menstrual seclusion (9–16 days) and for 3 days during next menses.[c]	
43	Reddiur (Montgomery 1972:114)	Girls are fed as well as family can afford for three months after first menstruation and thereafter during each menstrual period.	

Table 6—*continued*

Index no.[a]	Research site and source	Food	Medical care	Love
E	Thadagam, South Arcot District (Madras Village Survey Monograph 9 1964:14)	Special food is given to girls during their menstrual seclusion.		
F	Kunnalur, Thanjavur District (Madras VSM 11 1964:12)	Girls are fed special food during 15 days of menstrual seclusion.		
G	Sirumalai, Madurai District (Madras VSM 29 1967:19)	Girls are fed special strengthening nonvegetarian foods for 15 days of menstrual seclusion.		
H	Kilakotta, Tirunelveli District (Madras VSM 21 1965:12)	Girls are fed special foods like sweets, eggs for 16-day menstrual-seclusion period.		
I	Pudukulam, Tirunelveli District (Madras VSM 10 1964:11)	Girls are given delicious foods like eggs, meat for 16-day menstrual-seclusion period.		
J	Kadukkara, Kanya Kumari District (Madras VSM 13 1965:10)	Girsl are fed special foods during menstrual seclusion.		
K	Kadathuchery, Kanya Kumari District (Madras VSM 16 1965:9)	Girls are fed special foods during menstrual seclusion.		

L	Kotthuthal Azhamkulam, Kanya Kumari District (Madras VSM 19 1965:9)	Girls are given eggs and sweets for 7-day menstrual-seclusion period.
M	Nemmara, Palghat District (Kerala VSM B 1967:226)[d]	Pubescent girls are fed sweets.
N	Thalikulam, Trichur District (Kerala VSM B 1967:405)	Girls receive sweets during menstrual seclusion.
56	Ramankara (Fuller 1978)	No differences shown in amount of love given or time spent caring for girls and boys; affection tends to be lavished on youngest, to older children's resentment.

[a]Index numbers denote those sites of ethnographic research referred to in Table 1 and mapped in Figure 2. Sites referred to by a capital letter are not part of the basic corpus of studies used in this book but appear here because they provide important supplementary evidence on the topic.

[b]My thanks to Michael Moffatt of Rutgers University for providing me with this source.

[c]Feeding special foods to girls for a week or two probably has no effect, in itself, on the health and survival of females. But I think it is highly indicative of an attitude of solicitude concerning female health which is probably carried out in everyday feeding patterns.

[d]Most Village Survey Monographs on Kerala note that puberty rites were performed formerly but are not at present.

which discrimination against girls is reported are northern.[9] But, curiously, some instances of preferential feeding of girls were also found in the South. Clearly cultural rules regarding who is worth feeding are operative throughout South Asia, but they do not always favor males (Fig. 7). Montgomery (1972) describes a very nonnorthern pattern of food distribution in the Tamil village where he studied. Besides infants who are fed on demand, the only people who receive special food are pubescent girls (1972:114). Pubescent girls are fed as well as the family can afford for three months after the onset of menstruation and thereafter during every period. Preferential feeding of pubescent girls as a general South Indian practice is corroborated by many other studies and reports (Table 6).

Newell indicates that the Gaddis, of Goshen village of Chamba District in the northern hill region, give special snacks to girls and that girls are certainly not discriminated against in terms of food (1978). This is an important aberration from the plains pattern and fits with the sex ratio pattern that shows a marked break between the feminine juvenile sex ratios in the hills and the highly masculine sex ratios of the Gangetic plain. It can be no mere coincidence that favoritism toward girls in food distribution is found in Chamba District where survival for girls is also high. Thus the Himalayan region, while geographically northern, is in some cultural ways more akin to the South.

Medical Care

In exploring the question of whether there is significant variation in the kind and amount of medical care given to boys as compared with

9. Interesting evidence of male preferential feeding patterns also comes from Bangladesh, which though outside the geographical scope of this study, reflects on the findings for India. Lindenbaum describes a rating system whereby males are "worth" twice as much as females. This 2:1 ideology is carried over into food distribution: ". . . . mothers favour sons . . . and the male child receives preferential nutrition. Along with his father, he eats first; and if there is a choice, luxury foods or scarce foods are given to him rather than to his female siblings. The result is a Bengalee population with a proponderance of males and a demographic picture in which the mortality rate for females under 5 years of age is in some years 50% higher than that for males . . . a statistic not unrelated to the cultural code of right-left, two-one" (Lindenbaum 1977:143).

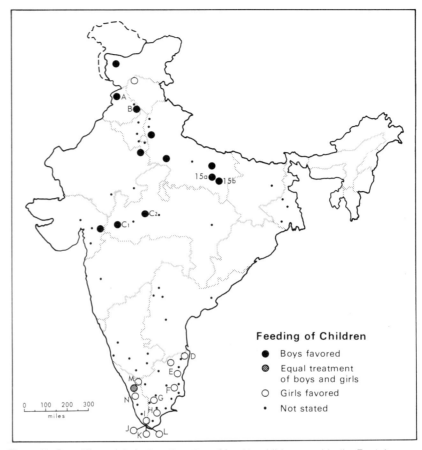

Figure 7 Sex differentials in the allocation of food to children, rural India. For information on sites, see Table 6.

girls in the North, I used two kinds of studies. The first is reports of hospital findings on certain diseases in India; often the authors of these indicate the sex ratio of the cases involved.[10] One would suspect

10. After reading articles on infantile diarrhea and other forms of morbidity in the Vellore area of Tamil Nadu (Jadhav and Baker 1961; Ahmed and Webb 1963; Lozoff et al. 1975), I was struck by the lack of reference to any male-female disparities. I wrote to Betsey Lozoff of Case Western Reserve University, inquiring whether sex disparities were actually nonexistent in morbidity or if, instead, they had merely not been studied. Lozoff kindly referred me to R. A. Feldman of the Center for Disease

that in the North more boys are taken to hospitals than girls as this kind of treatment is the most expensive and thus would be a scarce resource allocated to the favored offspring. It is important to remember that such reports do not necessarily tell us about sex ratios of *morbidity*—only sex ratios of children *taken for treatment*. The second kind of data is that of ethnographic reporting and questionnaire responses describing the nature of medical care allocated to children. This topic is a very important one since differentials in the allocation of medical care between boys and girls may be the crucial type of discrimination at work in North India (Leaf 1978). With increasing improvement of medical care and the widening of medical services, sex ratio imbalances already caused by better care to boys may widen, although there is some evidence to the contrary (Minturn 1976).

Looking first at the data from hospital reports, we see that hospital admissions in the North are heavily weighted in favor of boys, in the proportion of 2 or more boys to 1 girl (Table 7). The two examples from the South also show a majority of boys in hospital admissions but to a much less degree—only 1.2 boys to every 1 girl. The two studies from the central area (Bombay) both show a lower proportion of boys to girls than those from the North—1.5:1. These results from the North, compared with two examples from the South, while not conclusive proof that girls in the North are much more discriminated against in terms of good medical care than they are in the South, do provide one more indication that this is the case.

Just as the hospital reports from the North show greater imbalances

Control in Atlanta, Georgia, who was the head of the Vellore project. Feldman gave generously of his time in discussing my work with me and in offering much helpful criticism. He informed me that sex had not been considered as a variable in the Vellore morbidity study but that I could not conclude from this that there are no sex disparities in morbidity there. Feldman in turn referred me to P. S. S. Sundar Rao of Vellore Christian Medical Hospital, India. I wrote to Sundar Rao requesting his aid in discovering if there were sex differentials in hospital admissions at the Vellore hospital and if he was aware of any sex differentials in morbidity and mortality among children in the Vellore area. Sundar Rao replied with speed and much material, including sex ratios for both children and adults admitted to the Vellore hospital over many years and also some important unpublished data on mortality be sex and age in the Vellore area. In all, my gratitude to Lozoff, Feldman, and Sundar Rao is very deep.

Table 7
Number of hospital admissions of children and proportion of boys to girls, by city, 1962–1978

Location	Number of patients	Source	Proportion of boys to girls
Amritsar (Pun.)	105	Manchandra and Khanna 1962	2.2:1
Amritsar (Pun.)	1,846[a]	Manchandra and Sachdev 1962	2.6:1
New Delhi	500	Abraham et al. 1969	1.5:1
Allahabad (U.P.)	200	Pande 1976	2.4:1
Lucknow (U.P.)	110	Srivastava et al. 1973	1.3:1
Jabalpur (M.P.)	175	Sharma et al. 1968	1.8:1
Bombay (Mah.)	30	Kumbhat 1959	1.5:1
Bombay (Mah.)	300	Agrawal et al. 1969	1.5:1
	[b]	Agrawal et al. 1969	1.4:1
Vellore (T.N.)	[c]	Sundar Rao 1978	1.3:1
Thanjavur (T.N.)	365	Ramachandran and Purnayyam 1966	1.2:1

[a] These 1,846 patients represent only a fraction of the total number of child admissions (10,990) which the article discusses. The authors, however, do not give the proportions of boys to girls for the entire number of admissions, while the 1,846 subgroup is the largest for which they do.
[b] The total number of in-patients is not given.
[c] The total number of in-patients during 1972–1976 is 30,410.

in the numbers of boys and girls brought to the hospital for treatment, ethnographic reports of discrimination in favor of boys in the allocation of medical treatment are also preponderantly northern (Table 6 and Fig. 8). It is noteworthy that no southern ethnographer besides Beals reports sex differentials in medical care. This must mean that if such differentials exist (as shown by the slight male preponderance in Vellore hospital admissions) they are so slim as to escape notice. Beals's note on the lack of medical care given to girls *and* later-born boys is very revealing. Apparently both girls and later-born boys are less desired than are elder sons and are thus accorded less medical care.

The relationship between socioeconomic status and medical care of children is less clear. Both Marshall (1978) and Wadley and Derr (1978) note that there is less sexual discrimination in the upper strata. Minturn (1976) reports that whereas in 1954 Khalapur's population was 65 percent male, in 1974 it was 55 percent male, and she claims that the change is due to increased wealth in the village and better medical care available. Perhaps with increased wealth parents do give

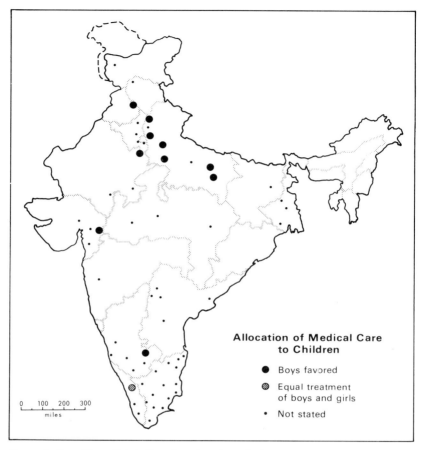

Figure 8 Sex differentials in the allocation of medical care to children, rural India. For information on sites, see Table 6.

better medical care to *both* boys and girls, but it is still too early to state anything definitive.

Love and Care

The third category of sexual discrimination investigated here is even more difficult to penetrate than the above two. Several major problems come to the fore when looking at differences in the allocation of love and care. First, we need to know if differences could be related to variations in survival, that is, can a lack of love actually prove fatal to a child? Second, there is great difficulty in obtaining data on the love and care given to children of either sex in Indian homes.[11] Third, it is hazardous trying to assess the impact of deprivation in terms of love as compared with nutritional or medical deprivation, for very often the three may go hand in hand.

There have been studies that point to a lack of *maternal* care and general poor health of the child concerned.[12] Jelliffe refers to this, paraphrasing Geber and Dean (1956):

> In some parts of the world such as Buganda, the child may be suddenly taken from the breast without preparation and sent to stay with a relative, often living a long way away. This can result in comparative neglect and in a form of "maternal deprivation" syndrome with such nutritionally relevant symptoms as anorexia and vomiting. [Jelliffe 1968:119]

Thus if a child becomes emotionally upset because of loss of contact with a primary love object, there can be repercussions on the child's nutritive intake and capacity to make use of the nutrients ingested which can be ultimately fatal. Expanding on the relationship between "maternal" deprivation and children's health, Jelliffe again paraphrases Geber and Dean:

> Not only is there a relationship between maternal deprivation and kwashiorkor but also speedier recoveries and lower mortality rates occur in children with kwashiorkor attended in hospital by affectionate mothers or kindly nurses, while the correlation of severity with the absence of the mother or maternal indifference is also recognized. [1968:131]

Beyond affecting a child's health through inadequate intake of nutrients which leads ultimately to kwashiorkor as mentioned by Jelliffe, love deprivation can also cause growth failure. In his very

11. For example, Mencher (1963), in an otherwise flawless article on child-raising techniques in Kerala, employs what is apparently the generic "he," "his," and so on. The reader is unsure whether such usage always refers to both boys and girls.

12. Early research on parental deprivation in children was focused almost completely on the effect of lack of *maternal* care. Such research has been resurrected by Fraiberg (1977) to support her argument that the mother is the most important figure for the child. Most other, more recent, research shows that, while a primary attachment figure is very important for a child's development, that figure need not be the child's biological mother (Birns 1978).

convincing article "Deprivation Dwarfism," Gardner (1972) presents results of his study of the effects of environmental and emotional deprivation on children's growth rates. The author concludes that dwarfism can result from a complex interplay of hormonal and brain impulses heavily affected by parent-child interaction. Though none of the children with whom Gardner worked were near fatality, their growth was seriously stunted and, if unattended, the children's conditions could have become very serious. In fact Gardner hypothesizes that emotional deprivation is perhaps "the underlying cause of the spectacularly high mortality rates in the 18th- and 19th-century foundling homes of Europe" (1972:76).

If in rural India a daughter were born when a son was ardently desired, is it possible that a mother might be so disappointed that she would unconsciously reject that daughter and thus give her less love and warmth than are necessary for proper growth and development? Failure to bear a son can result in the husband's taking a second wife—a very unhappy situation for the first wife—and can also be a cause of suicide among young wives (Marshall 1978). Certainly if lack of a son can warrant the taking of one's own life, it could also be related to great disappointment at the birth of a daughter, disappointment so severe as to affect that daughter's survival. This hypothesis is very difficult to prove and much of my evidence will be suggestive rather than conclusive.

The situation depicted by ethnographic evidence on love and care of boys versus girls is not as clear as that described by data on nutrition and medical care, but some sense can nevertheless be made of it (Table 6). Some researchers (Madan, Aggarwal, Marshall, and Newell) state that boys receive more love than girls; later-born "only" sons may be especially favored (Wadley and Derr). All these reports come from northern villages, but not all northern studies note such discrimination: Leaf reports that there are no sex differences in Shahidpur, as do Freed and Freed for Shanti Nagar. The only other report of no sex differences comes from Fuller based on his Kerala experience.

Parity, or the sequential order of birth, appears to be an important variable. It is very interesting that both Newell, reporting on the hill region in the North, and Fuller, reporting on Kerala villages in the

South, indicate a preferential allocation of affection to *younger* children. This evidence contrasts with Aggarwal's statement that in the Mewat area first-born sons are generally spoiled—a situation that no doubt exists in much of the North Indian plains region. Parity also has an effect on the feelings toward daughters for there is, in North India, a general desire for one daughter (Poffenberger 1975:96). Thus while the birth of a first or perhaps a second daughter is not a great tragedy, the birth of a third or fourth daughter might be. A family with one or two daughters may indeed lavish love and care on the girls who must, through rules of village exogamy, leave their natal home upon their marriage. Minturn and Hitchcock mention the sentimentality involved in the feelings about daughters who are just "temporary" members of their parents' homes. But there is also some negative feeling associated with the temporariness of daughters, expressed in the Hindi metaphor likening a daughter to a *ciriyā ki āngan*, or a "bird of the courtyard" who dips in only to snatch some grain and then disappear. There is the feeling that, since her natal family does not get to "keep" their daughter, they go to all the trouble of bringing her up just for another family's advantage. Thus there is, in the North especially, an attitude of sentimental, almost compensatory, "love" coupled with a feeling that the daughter does not really belong to her natal family.

The inconsistency in reporting on the allocation of love may reflect the inaptness of the category itself. Asking about love may mean asking about what people *say* about loving their children more than what people actually *do* in terms of loving their children. For example, Minturn and Hitchcock (1966:97) say that the Rajputs of Khalapur have a "sentimental" feeling of love toward daughters which they do not feel toward sons. But it is not clear how this feeling is acted out—does the love sentiment mean that daughters actually receive more time spent caring for them or more solicitous attention when they cry? Not necessarily.

Roy provides an important clue in understanding this matter in her book on the life of upper-class Bengali women. Concerning food as symbolic of love, she explains: ". . . in Bengal, and perhaps all over India, feeding is the principle technique of women, no matter what age they may be, to show affection and love to their men. Food is also used as a means to show the withdrawal of love. It is a very common technique for the husband to say he has no appetite if he wishes to punish his wife or mother. Children are rewarded and punished with food or the withholding of it" (Roy 1975:95). The same point can be gleaned from King's (1977) analysis of the social symbolism involved in food transactions described in the modern Hindi literature of North India. Serving someone has implications beyond the expression of love—it implies a certain power in the server of the food over the one who is served. This is clearly drama-tized in the common practice of not allowing a new wife in a joint family to serve food to her own husband for many years after her marriage. The husband's mother relinquishes this task only with great reluctance for it means a lessening of her power over her son.

If the allocation of food is used as an indicator for the giving of love, then the category of love obviously is the same as that of the first category of discrimination—food. Nevertheless, there are some facets of loving and caring for children which this definition will not expose, such as the amount of time spent holding or watching over a child. Information on these matters is far too scant at this time even to consider but future research could uncover more definitive patterns in the amount of love lavished on boys and girls throughout rural India.

6
Women's Work and Female Worth in Rural India

Economic roles of females have long been a subject of academic interest. Such interest generally extends in two directions: the first is toward discovering determinants for the existing sexual division of labor and the second aims at discovering how economic roles influence other facets of life. Efforts in the first direction will be reviewed here and briefly assessed as to their relevance to the situation in rural India. Later sections of this chapter and later chapters proceed in the second direction.

Anthropologists' theories of why male and female work roles differ are legion. They can best be examined by grouping them according to the factor—biological, economic, or cultural—which is given precedence in determining the division of labor. Many of the theories mentioned here incorporate more than one of these types of factors; note will be made of this where necessary.

One invocation of biology as the most important factor in the division of labor by sex comes from Brown (1970) who takes the female role of motherhood and its attendant child-care responsibilities as a constant demand on females in every culture. The prevailing type of economy is then the factor affecting variability in female labor participation. She explains this interrelationship between child-care responsibilities and the economy: ". . . in tribal and peasant societies that do not have schools and child-care centers, only certain economic pursuits can accommodate women's simultaneous child-care responsibilities" (1970:1077). The theory continues on that high rates of female labor participation will be found in societies in which economic tasks can be carried out near home, do not require much concentration, are not dangerous, and can be interrupted and then easily resumed. Therefore the major subsistence activity of a society, once the nature of its labor requirements are known, is the best "predictor" of women's labor participation (1970:1075).

The obvious weak point in Brown's argument is that child-care demands cannot be assumed to be universal in limiting the work participation of females. Variation in time spent on child care is vast, as are the alternatives employed in taking care of children in cultures where there are no schools or day-care centers. Oakley (1972:131– 135) points to many societies in which maternity and motherhood scarcely affect female productivity. Friedl (1975:8) takes us one step further in hypothesizing that, while there is indeed a relationship between childbearing and child-rearing patterns and women's work, the direction of influence is the opposite of what Brown suggests; that is, it is largely women's work that influences patterns of childbearing and care. On the basis of the ethnographic evidence it is clear that the biological act of maternity does not in itself seriously restrict female participation in production. Rather it is culture that creates serious restrictions by loading motherhood with particular inhibiting values.

Further, Brown's position does not enlighten the pattern of variation which will be presented for India. In India, within the same area where the major subsistence activity is similar throughout (for example, rice-growing areas of the East or South, or wheat-producing areas of the North), female labor participation varies tremendously according to social class. Thus a biological factor such as maternity cannot be used to explain variations in female labor participation rates in rural India.

"Mode of subsistence" is often cited as determining the sexual division of labor; for Friedl, it is "basic" (1975:7). Goldschmidt, in referring to the specific case of peasant societies, proposes that it is the peasant mode of production itself which defines sex roles in that context:

> The patriliny of peasant families is associated with the fact that men almost always are in charge of farming in peasant societies. This

probably derives from the fact that the circumstances of folk life deprive men of their earlier economic pursuits: war and hunting. For war (with few exceptions) is not a regular occupation of the peasants . . . and dense settlements make game scarce and hunting the sport of the privileged. [1959:206]

This highly speculative theory is resurrected by Goldschmidt and Kunkel (1971) in an article on male dominance in peasant society. Such a "deprivation" theory fails to explain differences in degree of masculine control of farming in different peasant economies, for example, differences between northern wheat farming and southern rice cultivation in rural India.

A more sophisticated analysis is done by Goody, who, leaning heavily upon Boserup (1970), discusses the differences in women's economic roles in relation to simple or shifting agriculture where the female role is great, as contrasted with plough agriculture where females are restricted largely to the domestic sphere (1976). No explanation for this pattern is proffered for he is more interested in discovering associations among female economic roles, property, and marriage, than in discovering determinants of the economic roles themselves.

Without going too deeply into the details of different types of agricultural economies and their demands for female labor, several points briefly can be made which are pertinent to the situation in rural India. First, there are basic differences between dry-field plough agriculture and intensive wet rice cultivation in terms of the relative inputs of labor from males and females; second, there are differences in the use of female labor under two types of riziculture, broadcasting and transplanting; third, some examples from India illustrate how cultural rules concerning the division of labor by sex affect the relative inputs of male and female labor in rice cultivation throughout the subcontinent with particular emphasis on differences between West Bengal and the South.

Differences in the labor demands and relative inputs of the two sexes between dry-field plough agriculture and wet rice cultivation have been succinctly summarized by Moore:[1]

1. Several authors point to the immense amounts of labor required for wet rice cultivation as opposed to dry-field cultivation (Béteille 1975:67; Bardhan 1974: 1293–1303; Mencher 1977).

Intensive rice contrasts with other major staple crops grown by peasant cultivators in that women play a very important role in its cultivation, a role usually approximately equal to that played by men. The major contributions of females to intensive rice cultivation are usually made in transplanting, weeding, and harvesting, although the latter is commonly shared with males. The pattern of labor requirements for intensive rice cultivation differs from that for alternative staple crops (e.g., millet, wheat, maize) under plough agriculture . . . in that the ploughing operations, which in virtually every culture are undertaken by men . . . form only a relatively small proportion of agricultural operations (as measured in labor time) in the former case. In dry cereal cultivation, ploughing operations . . . constitute a very large proportion of total agricultural operations. Thus in dry cereal cultivation the role played by women in agriculture is necessarily small. [1973:912]

Moore thus combines the general labor requirements of the two types of agriculture with cultural rules regarding the division of labor—that females rarely do ploughing operations—and devises a broad formula for the relative input of female labor. In a response to Moore, Winzeler (1974) accepts the importance of the mode of production and its labor requirements but adds a dash of sophistication to the argument: "The implications of wet rice cultivation for social organization appear to vary under different conditions; in order to draw causal inferences about wet rice cultivation it would seem necessary to specify a number of intervening variables including kinship patterns, population density and, perhaps, cultural traditions" (1974:564). Winzeler's advice is pertinent to the Indian situation where no single factor, such as type of agricultural economy, can be taken as the determinant of female labor participation.

An important contrast must now be drawn between the varying inputs of females in two different kinds of rice cultivation: transplanting and broadcasting. The former is a very intensive method requiring large inputs of labor while the second is less intensive and requires much less labor. Hanks describes these two types of riziculture in almost poetic terms but unfortunately gives few facts concerning the amounts of labor required by each (1972:33–39). By reading between the lines, one discerns that several operations required in the transplanting type are circumvented when the broadcasting method is employed: diking of the fields, extra fertilization, much weeding, and careful regulation of water level, besides the onerous task of trans-planting the seedlings. Since weeding and transplanting are often female tasks, broadcasting appears to require less female labor than transplanting. Let us now consider some examples from rural India which highlight the importance of cultural regulation of the sexual division of labor in two different rice-growing areas—West Bengal and the South, especially Kerala and Tamil Nadu.

The situation in the far South conforms more closely to Moore's depiction of the labor demands of intensive rice cultivation than does West Bengal. In Kerala and Tamil Nadu where rice is cultivated intensively, females form an important part of the labor force (Men-cher 1977). In South Kanara District (in Karnataka), which adjoins northern Kerala and is socially and culturally more akin to Kerala than to the rest of Karnataka, Claus notes that in rice cultivation there (transplanting method) "the role of the female in the cultivation of the household's fields is equal to or slightly greater than that of the male" (1970:42). In fact, in this district the number of females forms a larger proportion of the agricultural labor force than does the number of males (1970:43). The activities of manuring, transplanting, har-vesting, threshing, winnowing, and husking of the paddy are all performed exclusively by women (1970:43). The great importance of women as agricultural workers is dramatized by the fact that a com-mon measure of land is in terms of the number of women required to work it. Mencher (1977) also reports on the importance of women in rice cultivation in certain areas of Kerala where garden cultivation (of coconuts and so forth) is done mainly by males and rice cultivation mainly by females.

This forms a stark contrast to the sexual division of labor in rice cultivation in West Bengal. Here transplanting is often a male task, as are most of the other operations except for the husking of the paddy which is the reserve of females. A photograph of males engaged in rice transplanting in a West Bengal Village Survey Monograph (No. 3) is a strange sight to one familiar with the same situation in the South. In addition to cultural rules regarding the sexual division of labor, another factor works to reduce the participation of females in rice cultivation in West Bengal: a greater use of the broadcasting method than elsewhere, in proportions of one-half broadcasting to one-half transplanting (Greenough 1982). Deltaic conditions in West Bengal require smaller amounts of labor in order to obtain a paddy crop as the flood waters help to keep weed growth to a minimum, provide the necessary moisture for the fields without irrigation, and bring nourishment to the seedlings at the same time. Again the female task is the husking of the paddy and even this is being usurped increasingly by machines.

In West Bengal, as contrasted with the South of India, the growing of rice is considered to be a valuable task and is reserved for the males. One author (Davis 1975:169–170) associates the greater value attached to the male sex in West Bengal with the fact that males grow the rice and thus provide the source of sustenance, strength, and well-being for all.

There is obviously nothing intrinsic to the operations of rice cultivation which require specifically *female* labor. Rather it is culture that defines sexual roles and culture can be very arbitrary.

The importance of cultural factors in affecting female labor participation has been occasionally emphasized. Papanek discusses how the traditional practice of purdah, or the seclusion of women, in Pakistan both retards and fosters change in female labor participation. While purdah prevents women from entering into occupations where they would have direct contact with unknown males, it at the same time creates the development of a female clientele for female doctors and teachers (1971:522). Dixon (1978), in speaking of purdah throughout the area stretching from North Africa through the Middle East to South Asia, also points to its limiting aspect in terms of female participation in labor. In an analysis of female participation in the nonagricultural sector, Youssef analyzes census data from the Middle East (1971, 1974) and concludes that, in combination with available job opportunities for women, the joint cultural traditions of female seclusion and exclusion are major restricting influences on women's labor participation. The concept of the protection of family honor through the seclusion of females is central to her argument:

> In Middle Eastern societies, family standing depends largely, if not exclusively, upon conformity to behavioral norms that are conceived as having to do with 'male' honor. This honor is determined above all by the sexual conduct of a man's womenfolk: premarital chastity of

the daughter and sister, fidelity of the wife, continence of the widowed and divorced daughter or sister. . . . [1971:431–432]

In a microstudy focused on the Indian city of Chandigarh (Punjab), D'Souza examines the relationship between family status and female labor participation. He finds a curvilinear relationship between the two factors such that there is high female labor participation in the lower- and higher-status categories while low participation characterizes the middle-status families. The author's concluding comment is important:

> One may use the generalization that female work participation is determined by family status consistency to explain changes in the rate of female work participation in a given region and over a period of time, but it cannot provide an explanation of the variation in the rate among different regions, without taking into account important historical and cultural factors. [1975:141]

Cultural factors can and do influence female labor participation but they should not be viewed in isolation from the general economic system in which they are embedded. For instance, the question of the distribution of the purdah system should be tackled. Why is it not characteristic of Africa south of the Sahara? Why is it more prominent in northern India than southern India? The answer to these queries will probably be found in the differing nature of the productive systems of the areas concerned, because "sentiments" for and against women working are responsive to the needs of production.

Obviously there are many factors involved in shaping patterns of female participation in production throughout the world. The nature of production's demands for labor, the labor supply available, cultural definitions of who may work at which jobs—all these are important to varying degrees in different places and times. In rural India the pattern of female labor participation responds to all these factors, and more.

Female Labor Participation in Rural India

A major analysis of labor participation in India is Schwartzberg's study of 1951 Census of India occupational categories (1961); however, the author concentrates on male employment. Most of the published work on specifically female employment consists of brief articles which expose some of the broad regional differences in female work rates but offer few clues as to the significance of these (Nath 1968; Mukherji and Mehta 1975; Reddy 1975; Gulati 1975).[2] A more significant contribution is an essay entitled *Women in the Working Force in India* by Gadgil (1965) which devotes much space to a consideration of the rural scene. Gadgil correctly states that census data on female employment can lead to the formulation of the proper questions but that answers to such questions can be found only through intensive local studies. The two questions which he considers important are also the ones I consider most pressing: regional variation and social variation in female labor participation. He notes that, according to 1961 Census of India data, at the all-India level there are 50 female workers for every 100 male workers in cultivator (generally landed) families, but that among laboring (generally landless) families there are 82 females for every 100 male workers (1965:31).[3] The author cites some census figures showing that there is also social variation in the proportion of working females to males.

Unfortunately Gadgil's explanation for the regional and social variation in female labor participation is not as clearly put forth as the problem. This is due in great part to the paucity of the intensive local studies which he feels should be the source of any explanation. Thus Gadgil is led to speculate in rather grand terms. His major points are that female labor participation varies according to the demand for agricultural labor, and "sentiments" concerning female work. These are indeed crucial factors; Gadgil's fault lies only in not pursuing them further than he does.

Although I am not directly concerned with factors influencing female labor participation in rural India, but rather with how the latter influences other things, the question is important and should be addressed in the near future. It will suffice to state briefly here my opinion on the most important factors shaping both regional and social variation in female labor participation rates in rural India: the

2. Different authors and even different Indian censuses use varied formulas and definitions for determining female work rates. They will be explained when necessary.
3. The 1961 Census definition of "worker" is given in Appendix B.

demand for labor and the distribution of wealth. The demand for labor incorporates several variables such as the type of agriculture, intensity of irrigation, and presence or absence of a large labor supply. These would help to explain the regional pattern in female labor participation rates throughout rural India. The pattern of the distribution of wealth is also correlated with female work rates in village India, as wealth is an important factor determining whether female members of the family do field work. Looking at just one index of the distribution of wealth in rural India—that of land—there is a regional pattern in the distribution of landedness versus landlessness, such that landlessness is most widespread in the South (Schwartzberg 1961:179). The North is characterized by low and medium percentages of landlessness. Hence it is expected that high female labor participation will be found in the South where landlessness is more prevalent, and where poverty drives more women to work and inhibits the imposition of purdah by very many families.

Regional pattern. To study the regional aspect of the question, I employ 1961 Census of India data.[4] In the analysis to follow, the female labor participation rate (FLP rate, or, simply FLP) is defined as the number of working females aged 15–34 years as a percentage of all females aged 15–34 years. Only the rural population is considered. The limited age group of 15–34 was chosen because it is the age group in which the majority of working women are found.

The range of district-by-district variation is extremely wide (Fig. 9). It extends from a low of 1.7 percent in Pilibhit District in Uttar Pradesh to a high of 98.3 percent in the mountain district of Chamoli, also in Uttar Pradesh and indeed not very far from Pilibhit. The area of lowest FLP (under 41 percent, comprising one-third of all the districts) stretches from the Punjab to West Bengal. The southern state of Kerala also, surprisingly, falls into this category. What is most unexpected about this large set of low FLP districts is that it

---

4. The definition of work employed in the 1971 census was much stricter and greatly reduced numbers of women regarded as workers by the 1961 Census (Gulati 1975). Since my concern is whether women work in public or not (and not the number of days worked or amount of income gained) the 1961 data are better for my purposes.

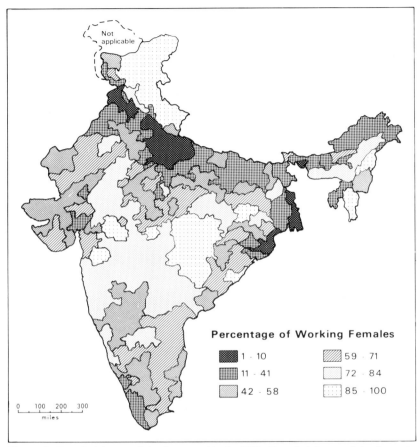

Figure 9 Female labor participation, rural India, 1961. Female labor participation rate is the number of working females aged 15–34 years as a percentage of all females aged 15–34. Note: The normal symbolization in which light shades denote low values and dark shades denote high values is reversed here in order to highlight the relationship between juvenile sex ratios (Fig. 4) and female labor participation rate.

includes both wheat-producing areas (low female labor demand) and rice-producing areas (high female labor demand) where one would expect high and low FLP in the respective ecological regions on the basis of a simple demand theory.

Highest female participation is found in the mountain districts bordering on Tibet and in the internal hilly regions. Part of this pattern is consistent with expectations as these are areas of swidden cultivation and millet cultivation, both of which are often characterized by high inputs of female labor. The medium range of female participation is found in Gujarat in the West and much of the South.

An important question to be considered is whether there is a correlation between rates of female labor participation and juvenile sex ratios (JSR). According to my hypothesis there should be a close correlation between the two factors showing that the participation of females in production does affect the survival of females. A statistical test of correlation between women's work level and juvenile sex ratio for all rural districts of India, a total of 323, yields a correlation of .43 which is moderately strong and highly significant considering the number of districts involved (Fig. 10). The scatter diagram forms a very interesting pattern exhibiting a fairly clear upper boundary of decreasing values from the upper left-hand corner, where JSR is high and FLP is low, to the lower right-hand corner, where JSR is low and FLP is high. The upper right-hand area, where both the masculinity of the juvenile population and the working level of women would be high, is significantly empty. The scatter of dots on the lower left, where FLP is quite low yet sex ratios are still very feminine, consists mainly of rice-growing districts in the states of Kerala, West Bengal, Assam, and Orissa—a problem which will be addressed shortly. From the evidence at hand, we can draw a generalization about the covariation between JSR and FLP in rural India: where FLP is high, there will *always* be high preservation of female life, but where FLP is low, female children may *or* may not be preserved.

FLP and MLP

The low FLP for districts in Kerala is especially puzzling because 1961 Census figures show that in the class of landless laborers, female workers actually outnumber males in many districts. It is true that there are not so many women in the cultivating (landed) class recorded as working; nevertheless it seems that Kerala should not be in the predominantly northern category of low FLP.

It is a fact that Kerala has the highest rate of male unemployment of any state in India. The range of variation for MLP (male labor

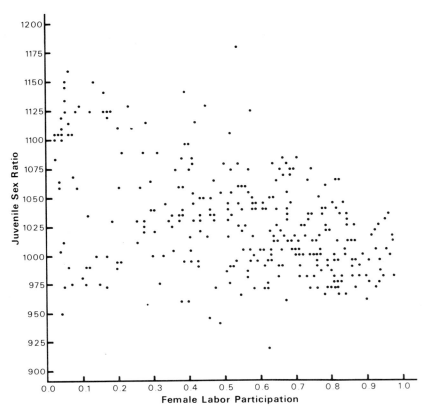

Figure 10 Correlation between juvenile sex ratio and female labor participation ratio, rural India, all districts, 1961. Juvenile sex ratio is the number of males per 1,000 females in the under-ten population. Female labor participation refers to the ratio of working females aged 15–34 years to all females aged 15–34 years.

participation rate, number of working males aged 15–34 as a percentage of all males aged 15–34 in rural India) is much narrower than that of FLP. It extends from a high of 98.2 percent in tribal Jhabua District of Madhya Pradesh to a low of 70.7 percent in Alleppey District in Kerala. Besides Manipur (MLP 77.0 percent), Goa (MLP 78.0 percent), and most of the districts in Kerala, there are no other rural districts with MLP below 80 percent. All districts of Kerala except for Cannanore (MLP 81.5 percent) and Palghat (MLP 85.6 percent) have MLP below 80 percent. Kerala is thus unique in rural

India for its low rate of male employment. Knowing this, I hypothesized that a situation of high unemployment for males would adversely affect female employment. The correlation between MLP and FLP for all Indian districts turns out, however, to be weak ($r = .18$). The two are too weakly related for variations in the one to account for variations in the other; variations in FLP must be associated with different factors entirely from those affecting male working levels. Another way of incorporating the markedly lower level of MLP in Kerala in the calculus is to measure the *disparity* between the rates of the two sexes. This measure, which modifies female labor rates according to the corresponding male levels, might help to bring Kerala and other rice-growing areas into line with our expectations that the demand for female labor is associated with a low juvenile sex ratio, in effect, shifting the scatter of points representing those districts toward the right on the scatter diagram.

The disparity between MLP rates and FLP rates was measured for all rural Indian districts using a disparity index developed by Sopher (1974, 1979). The disparity found ranges from an extremely high value of 3.069 in Pilibhit District, Uttar Pradesh, to a low value of $-.846$ in Tehri Garhwal District, Uttar Pradesh (negative male/female disparity indicates that the proportion of females working is greater than the corresponding proportion of males). Comparing the disparity values to those of FLP alone, several features are apparent. First, the two variables are closely, although negatively, correlated, as one would expect because of the large variation in the female rate compared with the male: where FLP rates are high, the disparity between male and female rates is low and vice versa. A test for correlation between FLP and the disparity between FLP and MLP yields the figure of $-.875$, an expected high negative correlation. Most districts remain in the broad division into thirds that has been used in describing the distribution of female work rates.

The most remarkable change is in the status of Kerala. Instead of the low to very low levels of FLP, most Kerala districts have lower than average disparity (Kozhikode being the only exception with disparity somewhat above average). Kerala, but not West Bengal and parts of Orissa, has become better aligned with the rest of the South. Using the disparity index, however, did not change the deviant status of certain other rice-producing areas such as West Bengal and Orissa. The problem that all rice-producing areas in India do not have similar FLP rates is a fascinating one, but its solution is not necessary for the present discussion since my concern here is with the relationship between work rates of females and their survival; therefore the question of rice production and work rates will be relinquished in favor of an examination of the relationship between juvenile sex ratios and disparity.

DIS and JSR

When we examine a slightly different relationship, that of disparity (DIS) and juvenile sex ratios, we find, surprisingly, that using the disparity rates instead of FLP failed to improve the earlier correlation; between DIS and JSR the correlation is .41 (Fig. 11). If one draws a line in Figure 11 horizontally at the juvenile sex ratio of 1,070 and another vertically at the mean disparity of .95, the four quadrants generated are revealing.[5] In the upper right are found several districts with high disparity and high sex ratios, as my hypothesis predicts. Most of these are districts in the Punjab, Haryana, and western Uttar Pradesh. In the lower right quadrant there are many districts with higher than average disparity but "normal" sex ratios. These are primarily districts in the states of West Bengal, Orissa, Andhra Pradesh, and Mysore. The upper left quadrant is also empty, as expected; these districts represent low sex disparity in work levels but high sex ratios and are found mainly in Rajasthan. In the lower left quadrant are districts with low labor rate disparity and low sex ratios, again in accordance with expectations; these are from Central India.

Thus we can say of the relationship between male/female disparity in work levels and masculinity of the juvenile population that where the former is low, the latter is *never* high; where the former is above average, however, there is no necessary relationship with juvenile sex ratios—they can be either high (as in the Punjab and Uttar Pradesh) or low (as in West Bengal and Orissa). Certainly there is no

---

5. The figure 1,070 was chosen because it is a generous upper limit of what can be considered nonsuspicious juvenile sex ratios.

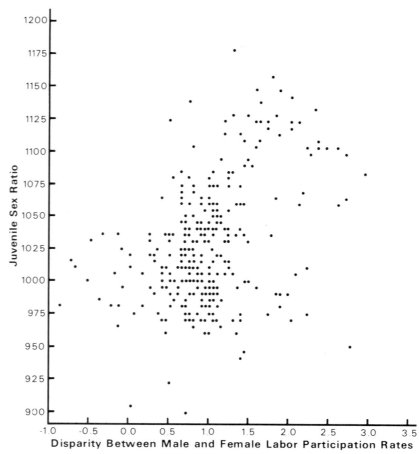

Figure 11 Correlation between juvenile sex ratio and the disparity between male and female labor participation rates, rural India, all districts, 1961.

strict one-to-one relationship between female work and female survival in rural India, but, on the other hand, the two factors are clearly related. An important facet of this relationship emerges from the pattern of residuals derived from the regression of the juvenile sex ratio on the male/female disparity in work levels (Fig. 12).

These residuals represent the remaining statistically unexplained variation in the juvenile sex ratio *after* the covariation with work-

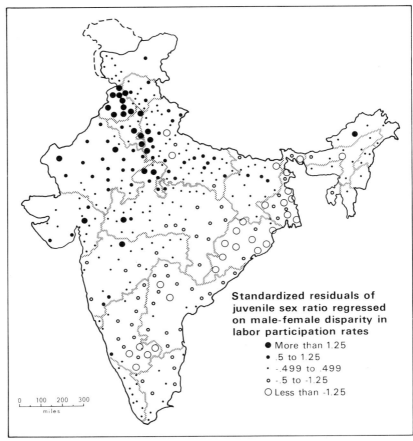

Figure 12 Residuals of juvenile sex ratio regressed on the disparity between male and female labor participation rates, rural India, all districts, 1961.

level disparity has been taken into account (assuming that the linear relationship established does so satisfactorily). There is a clear North-South pattern corresponding to the cultural-historical division of India noted in Chapter 1. The North is characterized by even higher juvenile sex ratios than one would predict given the high disparity in work rates there. This pattern is especially true of the Punjab and western Uttar Pradesh. In a broad, coherent band extending from West Bengal to the eastern border of Kerala the opposite situation prevails: even more girls survive than the low disparity predicts. In

the central zone, with low residuals, the juvenile sex ratios correspond to the values predicted by the parities in work levels.

This is an aspect of contrast between the North and the South
which is *not* explained by labor participation rates, for it is by holding
labor participation constant that this stark pattern emerges. The possibility that this pattern is related to *something* in wheat versus rice
cultivation cannot be easily dismissed, for the pattern of wheat cultivation roughly coincides with the residuals in the North while the
distribution of rice cultivation coincides with the band of residuals in
the South.

Some Checks

In order to allay doubts as to the accuracy of the overall pattern of
female labor participation in rural India, I consulted Village Survey
Monographs for three states—Uttar Pradesh, West Bengal, and Kerala. Uttar Pradesh was chosen because its FLP is reported in the census
to be extremely low and thus there might be an underenumeration of
female workers. I examined Kerala and West Bengal since they are
both rice areas with different rates of FLP, a difference that raises a
question. As a further test of the census data I compared findings
from ethnographies on Indian villages concerning FLP.

Village Survey Monographs. The villages studied in the monographs were not always chosen for their typicality or representativeness. The general introduction to each monograph explains the reason
for the selection of the particular village studied; the usual reasons are
that a particular caste is predominant, or a particular tribe, or because
the village has an "old and settled" character. Not all of the villages
described in the monographs are even entire revenue villages; some
are hamlets of a larger village, or the village itself may be very small.
For my purposes the most useful monographs were those done on
"old and settled" villages because these villages have a fairly large
population (over 500) and are inhabited by members of several
castes. In all there are twenty-six village studies in the Uttar Pradesh
series of Village Study Monographs.[6]

6. I rejected only one study, because the village was extremely small; it contained
less than twenty families (VSM 24).

According to the 1961 Census of India, FLP in rural Uttar Pradesh is low, especially in the western districts. In only a few districts of the eastern part of the state (Basti, Gorakhpur, Jaunpur, Pratapgarh, Rae Bareli, Allahabad, and Mirzapur) does FLP rise above 41 percent. Likewise, male-female disparity is above average throughout the state: it is extremely high in the western districts, somewhat lower in a central band of districts, and even lower farther east. This pattern is confirmed by information on FLP in the Village Survey Monographs (Fig. 13).

Very high FLP, even 100 percent, is reported in tribal villages of the hilly districts. Low rates are found in many "old and settled" and "varied" or "multi-caste" villages. The range reported in all the monographs extends from 2.1 percent in a village in Aligarh District to 100 percent in the tribal villages. The Census of India also reports an extreme range of variability for the state, which, it will be remembered, has the districts with both the maximum and the minimum FLP for all of rural India. Figure 13 shows the villages studied, grouping them according to whether the FLP is high (72 percent and over), medium (42–71 percent), or low (41 percent and under).[7] Eight of the ten villages with low FLP are in the western part of the state. Five of the seven villages with high FLP are in the mountain districts; the remaining two are in the southeast. In spite of this rather irregular sample of villages, a pattern clearly emerges with low FLP in the west and higher FLP in the east. Highest FLP is found at the perimeter of the state, especially in the hill region, as expected. These studies clearly confirm the census data, for Uttar Pradesh at least.

The six Village Survey Monographs available on West Bengal are very inconsistent in terms of data provided and the quality of the data. In only three volumes were any data on FLP provided and these are not organized according to age categories as the U.P. data are.[8] The two "old and settled" villages are both reported as having no female workers, excluding some handicrafts work pursued at home. This

7. These categories are taken from the all-India range as presented in Figure 9.
8. The villages in the West Bengal series for which some data are provided are: Raibhagini of Bankura District (VSM 4), Chandrabhag of Howrah District (VSM 12), and the tribal village of Bhumij Dhan Sol, in Midnapore District where 88 percent of the women are reported to be workers (VSM 5).

Figure 13 Female labor participation in Uttar Pradesh, 1961. Female labor participation is calculated as noted in Figure 10. "Low" is 0–41 percent, "medium" is 42–70 percent, and "high" is 71 percent and above. Numbers refer to those of the 1961 Census of India Village Survey Monographs for Uttar Pradesh used in the analysis.

does accord with the low FLP for many districts but by no means stands as confirmation of the census data. Indeed the West Bengal data are quite erratic compared with those of other states, and may be less trustworthy. It is extremely unfortunate that the quality and quantity of Village Survey Monographs for West Bengal is so poor.

The last check using Village Survey Monographs was done on the state of Kerala, another rice-producing area, but one with a very different FLP pattern than West Bengal's. According to the census data,

FLP in Kerala ranges near 30 percent, much higher than West Bengal's percentage which is primarily in the teens or below, but still lower than what one would expect for a rice-producing area. In seeking either to affirm or to contradict the census data, we are again greeted by disappointment. Research on the twenty-six villages represented in the Kerala series of Village Survey Monographs, which are of quite high quality, yields very inconsistent results. The range of rates of labor participation among females aged 15–34 extends from a low of 7 percent to a high of 80 percent. Both of these rates come from villages in which most of the inhabitants are not engaged in agriculture but instead work in businesses in nearby towns. Rates from agricultural villages show no consistent pattern. Further, there is no regional pattern; nearby villages in the same district have very different rates of FLP. Therefore it may be pure coincidence that the median rate of FLP for all the villages was 36 percent, which does match the census figures. Considering the great variability between villages, these data cannot be said either to confirm or to refute the 1961 Census in any strong sense.

Ethnographic reports. I consult ethnographic reports here for two reasons: first, to examine the regional pattern to see whether it is consistent with the census pattern; second, to explore social variations in FLP.[9] For the purposes of this analysis, I have divided the rural population into two broad classes: the propertied and the unpropertied. As was mentioned in Chapter 3, the translation of a caste into one of these classes introduces a certain amount of error for such a translation tends to idealize a caste as a homogeneous class in relation to property, something which no caste ever is. I hope, however, that in the long run such errors cancel each other out (and that someone else will be inspired to improve on this awkward system).

9. Differences in FLP between females of different social classes could be investigated fruitfully through an all-India district-level comparison of work rates of females of the agricultural laboring (landless) class with those of females of the cultivating (landed) class in the 1961 Census of India. An alternate route is using FLP rates of the Scheduled Castes and Tribes as compared with those of the non-Scheduled population in the 1971 Census of India.

Table 8

Female labor participation among propertied and unpropertied groups, by research site

Index no.[a]	Research site and source	Propertied groups[b]	Unpropertied groups
2	Goshen (Newell 1978)	High: females at age 6 work in fields; cooperative work gangs include women.	
A	Sokoh, Kangra District (Bhalla 1964–1965: 44–85)	Medium: Rajput women do not work in fields; Girth women do.	
3	Shahidpur (Leaf 1978)	Low: Jat women do mostly domestic work.	
4	Dhara (Morrison 1965: 55, 74)	Low: women do no field work.	High: landless labor includes women of lower castes.
5	Badipur (Miller 1975: 93, 163)	Low: Brahman and wealthy Jat women do not work in fields.	High: Chamar women work in fields, Chuhra women work as sweepers.
6	Rampur (Lewis 1965:51)	Low: women do mostly domestic work.	
7	Shanti Nagar (Freed and Freed 1976:70–73)	Low: Brahman and Jat women do mostly domestic work.	
8	Chavandi Kalan (Aggarwal 1978)	High: Meo women work in fields.	
B₁	Upper Jamuna Khadir region (Chauhan 1966:97)	Low: women do not work in fields.	
11	Bunkipur (Marshall 1978)	High: Thakur and other women help in fields in busy season.	
B₂	Lower Hindan Khadir region (Chauhan 1966:268)	High: women of "owner" class work in fields.	
12	Karimpur (Wadley and Derr 1978)	Low: high-caste women do not work in fields.	High: low-caste women do field work.
13	Mohana (Majumdar 1958:187–188)	Low: high-caste women do not work in fields.	High: women work in fields.
15	Senapur (Luschinsky 1962:479–544); Madhopur (Cohn 1954:91–92)	Low: Thakur women do not work in fields.	High: Chamar women work as laborers.

Table 8—*continued*

Index no.[a]	Research site and source	Propertied groups[b]	Unpropertied groups
C	Sujarupa, Udaipur District (Carstairs 1975:233)	High: Rajput women work in fields with husbands.	
17	Awan (Gupta 1974:48)	Low: high-caste women do no field work.	High: poor women are part of labor force.
19	Samiala (Fukutake et al.:15)	Low: high-caste women do not work in fields.	
23	Nimkhera (Jacobson 1970:22)	Low: women in strict purdah (largely upper class) do no field work.	
25	Bharko (Shukla 1976: 126–127)	Low: high-caste women do not work in fields.	High: women work at paddy cultivation for wages.
26	Supar (Fukutake et al.:127)	Low: upper-class women do not work.	Medium: former women's work of hulling rice being taken over by machines; many women unemployed.
32	Shamirpet (Dube 1967:170–175)	Low: upper-class women do no field work.	High: women work in fields.
34	Six villages (Reid 1978)	Low: women do mostly domestic work.	
35	Totagadde (Harper 1958:12, 16; Wiltse Harper 1971:31–35)	Medium: Havik women do not work in fields but Divaru women do.	
36	Three villages (Claus 1970:42–45)	High: female role in rice cultivation equal to or greater than male's.	
38	Rampura (Srinivas 1976:137, 179)	Low: women generally remain in home.	High: most Harijan women work for wages.
40	Elephant (Beals 1974:51, 95)	High: women contribute substantially to family income.	High: women are needed to help in fields.
41	Olappalaiyam (Beck 1972:10, 32)	High: women oversee fields; even wealthiest women help.	

Table 8—*continued*

Index no.[a]	Research site and source	Propertied groups[b]	Unpropertied groups
43	Reddiur (Montgomery 1972:80–83)	Medium: women are important in cultivation when holdings are not large.	
45	Thaiyur (Djurfeldt and Lindberg 1975:113)		High: most Harijan women are engaged in cultivation.
46	Endavur (Moffatt 1978)		High: women make definite contribution to family income as laborers.
47	Parangudi (Moffatt 1978)		High: women make definite contribution to family income as laborers.
48	Sripuram (Béteille 1962:107, 125–127)	Low: most male landowners do not cultivate so it is inferred that wives do not either.	High: women do much of rice cultivation.
49	Thygasamuthiram (Sivertsen 1963:78)	Medium: Brahman and richest Shudra women do not work in fields but others do.	High: women hire out as agricultural laborers.
51	Tengalapatti (Dumont 1957b:86, 92, 211)	High: Pramalai Kallar women help in fields at harvest.	
56	Ramankara (Fuller 1976:32)	Low: only in poorest families do Nayar women work on land.	
58	Two fishing villages (Klausen 1968:80)	Low: only in very poor families do women work.	

[a]Index numbers denote those sites of ethnographic research referred to in Table 1 and mapped in Figure 2. Sites referred to by a capital letter are not part of the basic corpus of studies used in this book but appear here because they provide important supplementary evidence on the topic.

[b]The assignment of ratings to "high," "medium," and "low" categories is not made on the basis of statistics given by the authors on working women as compared with nonworking women. Rather, I assigned the rating on the basis of my interpretation of the ethnographic evidence available (which was often very scant). If women were reported as doing only domestic work, the rating given is "low." If it appears that many women of the village do work outdoors while many others do not, the rating is "medium." If most or all women work, even if only at certain times of the year, the rating is "high." Accuracy of ratings is thus questionable, for they depend on the detail presented by the authors and my adeptness at translating that information into ratings.

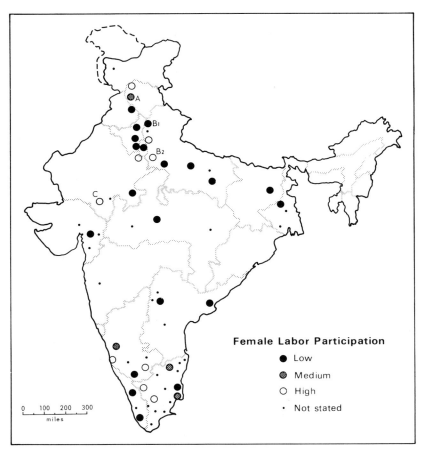

Figure 14 Female labor participation among propertied groups, rural India. For information on sites, see Table 8.

Rates of female labor participation among propertied groups show considerable variation throughout India and also among particular regions (Table 8, Fig. 14). High, medium, and low rates of participation are found in both the North and the South. Generally, the North has preponderantly low or medium participation rates, as does the South. Reports of high FLP from the North are from the Himalayan region, Rajasthan, and also from the Gangetic plain. Only villages in the last of these regions refute expectations for that area. In the South

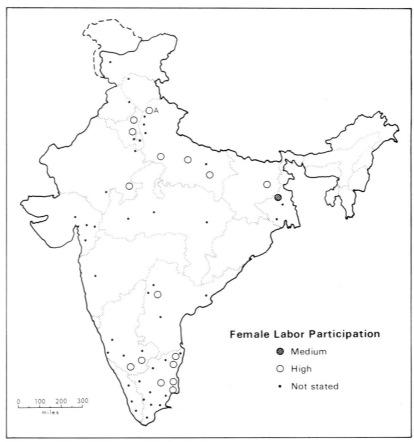

Figure 15 Female labor participation among unpropertied groups, rural India. For information on sites, see Table 8.

there are five clear cases of high FLP of women of the propertied class. The picture presented in the ethnographic data is of medium to low FLP among upper-class females all over India, with higher participation in the South standing as a clear counter-pattern. In contrast, the evidence on FLP among women of the unpropertied groups shows a consistent pattern throughout the North and South of high rates of participation (Table 8, Fig. 15). Most cases are of high FLP, as one expects from some studies (Mencher 1977; Béteille 1975; Nath

1968); it is unfortunate that there are not more reports available on the subject.

Any correlation between female labor participation and juvenile sex ratios on the social dimension can be accomplished only roughly at this time because the data are sparse and my interpretations of them open to question. The chart below portrays the relationships under consideration:

Class	Region	FLP	JSR
Propertied	North	Low	High
Propertied	South	Low-medium-high	Low
Unpropertied	North	High	Medium
Unpropertied	South	High	Low-medium

According to the hypothesis, a high demand for and use of female labor will support the survival of females and thus produce a low sex ratio, and should be found among the unpropertied groups, while among the propertied groups there will be found a low demand for and use of female labor with resulting sex ratios favoring males. Only two social categories delineated above fit this formula: the northern propertied groups and the southern unpropertied groups. Southern propertied groups have FLP rates ranging from high to low but their juvenile sex ratios are never high. Northern unpropertied groups, the other deviant category, have high labor participation rates but only medium juvenile sex ratios. Thus it appears that southern propertied groups "overpreserve" some economically "useless" females while northern propertied groups "underpreserve" economically "useful" ones.

7
Marriage Costs and Sex Ratios

If one were to ask a Jat farmer of the Punjab why too many daughters are a burden, one would not be told that it is because many females are not needed for wheat cultivation; rather the answer undoubtedly would be that it is costly to get daughters married. In a discussion of dowry-giving in Greece, Friedl brilliantly points out that an essential family obligation is to seek a balance between the amount of family property and the number of offspring (1959:49). Throughout rural India, culture devises many solutions to this problem both in the ways in which property is manipulated and in the ways the number of heirs is adjusted. Property is generally divided into immovable and movable property. In rural India males largely inherit the former and females the latter. Males thus inherit land—either at marriage or at their fathers' deaths. Females inherit their share in the form of goods and money primarily upon their marriage and have very little claim on the natal estate after that time.

Just as cultural rules mandate who receives what type of property, they can also distinguish between heirs and the disenfranchised in several ways. One system is through primogeniture which gives all rights to property to the first offspring (usually male) and simply provides nothing for subsequent offspring. The demographic effects of primogeniture may be migration of younger children or their remaining in the family as an unmarried member. In South India, the Namboodiri Brahmans of Kerala are a famous example of an elite

133

group practicing primogeniture (Mencher 1966). Ultimogeniture (which gives rights of inheritance to the youngest son) accomplishes approximately the same result in terms of keeping property intact and promoting migration among older siblings. A modified system of ultimogeniture occurs among the Nayars of Ramankara (Fuller 1976:64). According to this practice, the last child of either sex to marry has the responsibility of looking after the parents in their old age, and, after their deaths, inherits the parental home.

These examples provide only a scant taste of the wide variety of cultural rules that affect heirship and only a hint at some of the demographic effects brought about by them. This chapter explores the rule that, in northern Indian upper-class families particularly, daughters at their marriage must be given a large segment of family wealth in the form of dowry. It is my hypothesis that this necessity is a prime motivation for families wanting as few daughters as possible in order that a "balance" be maintained between the integrality of the family estate and claims to that estate from daughters (through dowry). Therefore where dowry is the custom and the practice, the high masculinity of sex ratios will express the devaluation of daughters.

Upon entering the realm of marriage payments we are immediately ensnared by emic-etic confusion. Studies of marriage payments which explain why a particular type exists in a particular society focusing only on emic interpretations are found on one end of the continuum, while analyses which completely ignore the emic aspect are situated at the other extreme. Unfortunately there is little in between. In a recent work, Pryor devotes one section to this problem of "subjective" (emic) and "objective" (etic) perceptions; he makes a case study of marriage payments to illustrate the problem and his remarks are revealing:

> Ethnographers have paid considerable attention to marriage payments and have recorded a wide variety of rationalizations supplied by informants as to why particular customs exist in different societies. For instance, a brideprice is supposed to represent a compensation for the mother's pain in bearing a child, the cost of bringing up the child (called "upfostering costs" in England), the loss of labor power to the natal family as a woman moves to the family of her husband, the price

of assigning any children of the marriage to the husband's family, and so forth. These rationalizations are not consistent between societies; for example, while in many societies the prospective wife's father graciously accepts a brideprice, in some societies this is expressly forbidden. . . . I developed a typology of such explanations and tried to code them for analytic purposes, but difficulties arose in coding because in many ethnographies it is unclear whether the "explanation" of the brideprice was that of the native informants or that of the ethnographer; experiments with such a variable finally had to be abandoned. [1977:367]

I agree with Pryor that in order to theorize about marriage payments or perform cross-cultural analyses of them, it is necessary to abandon the subjective and cleave to the objective. Goody's suggestions as to the important questions concerning marriage payments are instructive here; he feels the major questions are (1) size of payments, (2) use to which payments are put, (3) content or form of payment, (4) returnability, and (5) degree of variability (Goody 1973:3–14).[1] With the delineation of these concerns Goody has helped to place future studies of marriage payments on solid ground.

For the study of marriage payments in rural India undertaken here, it is impossible and unnecessary to take all the above questions into account. It is impossible because the data are simply not there in the ethnographies. It is unnecessary because the primary concern of this chapter is to assess how serious the burden of a daughter is on family finances, as compared with a son. Therefore I focus on the *type* of marriage payment, particularly dichotomized as dowry and brideprice.[2] Dowry, especially among upper-class families, is a great expense to the bride's family; bridewealth, obviously, is not. Another way of looking at the different burdens to a family in marrying a son versus a daughter is to determine whether the bride's or groom's side pays more in terms of overall marriage expenses, including feasts and

1. Although Goody (1973) mentions these questions in reference to the study of brideprice, they apply equally well to that of dowry.

2. Along with Goody (1973:1) I do not perceive dowry and brideprice as exact opposites of each other. Brideprice passes from the groom's family to the bride's family while dowry generally goes from the bride's family to the married couple themselves. (These definitions, however, do not always apply to the Indian situation.)

so forth.[3] The consideration of just these two points concerning marriage payments in rural India necessarily excludes much fascinating data on the content of the payments, the range of variability, and rules concerning returnability. But a narrow focus is both necessary and sufficient for the analysis of the problem at hand.

The Costs of Marriage

Considering the immense amount of ethnographic reporting on marriage in South Asia, it is amazing that the lack of synthetic works on the subject is so great. The prominent theoretician on Indian kinship, Dumont (1961, 1964, 1966), has written several articles on marriage in the North and South of India, but has little to say about regional or social variation in marriage payments beyond mentioning the fact that dowry is not universal throughout India (1959).[4] Karve's report on regional patterns of Indian kinship (1968), though methodologically questionable, does point to some of the major differences in inheritance forms and marriage payments found in various areas of India.[5] Still, Dumont's call more than twenty years ago (1957c) for careful comparative work on all aspects of Indian kinship has thus far been answered in the realm of marriage and marriage payments by only one researcher: Tambiah (1973). Standing far above any work on the subject of marriage payments in South Asia is his lengthy essay "Dowry, Bridewealth and the Property Rights of Women in South Asia." In this work the author unites a use of ethnographic studies

3. Before continuing, I should delimit the term "marriage payments." Strictly speaking, in the Indian context, the term should refer to the entire spectrum of costs involved in the marrying of an offspring. This would include travel expenses in search of a suitable spouse, engagement fees, various feasts before, during, and after the wedding, and any gifts given to the bride by her natal family in years following the wedding, which may often be substantial. But as difficult as it is to collect adequate data on the amount of dowry or brideprice, it is even more difficult to obtain specifics on this entire range of costs. Thus my use of "marriage payments" will be generally limited to the costs surrounding the wedding itself. As Tambiah notes, these constitute what can be considered the core of marriage payments in the wider sense and thus they capture the essence of the situation (1973:105).

4. Dumont's goal is to prove that India is "structurally" one; thus in all of his work he minimizes differences throughout the subcontinent.

5. For other criticisms of this work see Dumont (1957c).

and legal sources on inheritance with a flair for creative thinking to create a persuasive argument that India is a land where female rights to property are loudly proclaimed and largely actualized. His major contribution in the process of unfolding the argument is a clarification of some of the major similarities and differences between bridewealth and dowry. It will become obvious in the following analysis how large is my debt to Tambiah's work.

But there is one important issue upon which Tambiah and I disagree: the significance of regional and social variation in types of marriage payment. For my model, North-South differences are of paramount importance, as are differences between the upper and lower social classes. Tambiah chooses to dismiss such differences as less important than the overall similarity throughout South Asia: the recognition of female property rights through the concept of *strīdhan*, female wealth. It is my contention that it is impossible to prove that the concept is universal in South Asia, and that even if it should be universal, the acting out of the concept varies widely throughout the subcontinent. For Tambiah's argument to work, dowry (which he tends to equate with stridhan) must be the general form of marriage payment and it must represent wealth that *stays under the control* of the female involved. Neither of these prerequisites is completely met throughout India. First, other forms of marriage payment and marriages involving no payment whatsoever are statistically preponderant in India. Second, in many instances in northern India, a large part of a woman's dowry does not remain under her control. Cash especially may go to the groom's family and be used in turn to provide a dowry for a daughter in that family. Therefore the actualization of the concept of stridhan cannot be said to characterize all of India.

In order to impress the reader with the importance of dowry in India, Tambiah continually belittles both the frequency and character of bridewealth. Quoting the frequencies of type of marriage payments which Madan found in his study of the Brahmans of Utrassu-Umanagri village in Kashmir—38 percent of the dowry type, 45 percent of the exchange type involving minimal payments, and 17 percent of the bridewealth type—Tambiah states that this pattern represents in microcosm "the Indian situation" and illustrates the predominance of dowry over bridewealth even when the two coexist

(Tambiah 1973:70). Unfortunately for Tambiah this example instead indicates that dowry is not the main form of marriage type, for exchange marriages are in the majority. Tambiah would have done better to go to the Gangetic plain, for example, where percentages of dowry are higher! Besides trying to exaggerate the spread of dowry in terms of its frequency, Tambiah attempts to prove that even where dowry is not the custom, people feel that it is superior and thus are possessed of the concept of stridhan even if they don't practice it. In this way he seeks to show that dowry is everywhere the preferred form and bridewealth a surreptitiously carried out, inferior form. Speaking almost as if he were a Braham ideologue, he says that "by and large in India it is dowry that is publicly and ideologically and morally validated, and brideprice that is considered the 'degraded' and immoral form" (1973:71). True, the Brahmanical form of marriage with dowry is often considered more prestigious and when castes attempt to upgrade themselves they frequently assume this form of marriage payment, although on a smaller scale. But to insist that bridewealth is an "immoral" form is to express an upper-class view. Surely, the Udaiyar, a wealthy peasant caste of Tamil Nadu who claim never to have taken or given dowry even though they are aware that other groups do so, do not feel degraded or immoral about their customs—one senses, on the contrary, a feeling of pride in their own ways (Burkhart 1969:220). Another such example is that of the Holeru, a group of landless laborers of Karnataka studied by Harper (1968). The Holeru caste council recently tried to reduce the amount of bridewealth paid (Rs. 101) but their efforts were met with resistance since many Holeru feel that giving or taking less than the traditional amount is degrading to both families (1968:62). If the Holeru felt that giving bridewealth were immoral or degraded such resistance would probably not have been expressed. The Udaiyar and the Holeru provide just two counter-examples to Tambiah's argument. In the following section these and other examples from all over India, from high castes and low, will be used to provide a foil against Tambiah's constant diminution of the significance of non-Brahmanical forms and practices.

Type of Marriage Payment

Information on marriage payments from ethnographic reports is the only source of data used in this section and its use was not unproblematic. First, it is often unclear whether the author of a report is recording payments for just one or two marriage ceremonies witnessed while in the field or if "typical" or "average" payments for the entire group or village are provided. I treat all reports as if they are of the latter type. Second, it is often difficult to discern what the villager considers to be dowry or bridewealth, as the indigenous terms for these are rarely provided by the author with an explanation of their meaning. As Dumont notes, the dowry or bridewealth payment can form part of a continuous chain of prestations and counter-prestations between the bride's and groom's families so that it is impossible to separate one payment and call it the "dowry" or the "bridewealth" (1957a:31). This problem appears, however, to be more acute in the case of southern marriages. In some instances there were gifts recorded which bore resemblances to dowry or bridewealth but were not so termed by the author. The reader is left wondering if this absence is the result of the author's lapse or if the villagers do not themselves consider the payments to be either dowry or bridewealth.

Table 9 presents data from the ethnographies on type of marriage payment among propertied groups and unpropertied groups. Mapping the type of marriage payment is particularly difficult because of the complexity of the situation. In Figure 16, two simple categories of "bridewealth" and "dowry" were inadequate and even the five categories employed are an idealization. The first category, dowry, indicates that (according to the ethnographer) dowry is *the* form of marriage payment among that group. The second, bridewealth, refers to groups who are simply described as bridewealth givers. The next category refers to different marriage payments being made by different groups within one village (some give dowry, others bridewealth). The fourth category denotes the exchange of both bridewealth and dowry at a wedding, a form I call "Southern dowry."[6]

6. This mixed situation may be indicative of a transitional phase in which bridewealth payments are moving toward dowry, as Cohn suggests is the case among the Chamars of Madhopur (1972:75). However, in the South, the combination of gifts and payments from both sides appear to be traditional and not a product of Brahmanization.

Table 9

Type of marriage payment and family bearing greater marriage costs in rural India, propertied and unpropertied groups, by research site

Index no.[a]	Site and source	Propertied groups		Unpropertied groups	
		Type of marriage payment	Family bearing greater costs	Type of marriage payment	Family bearing greater costs
1	Utrassu-Umanagri (Madan 1965:114–115)	38% dowry, 45% exchange, 17% bridewealth			
2	Goshen (Newell 1965: 59–60; 1978)	No payments as such from either side	Groom's		
3	Shahidpur (Leaf 1972: 37, 190; 1978)	Dowry—no admitted bridewealth			
5	Badipur (Miller 1975: 148)	Dowry		Chamars give dowry	
6	Rampur (Lewis 1965: 162)	Jats give dowry	Bride's		
7	Shanti Nagar (Freed 1971; Freed and Freed 1976:79)	Dowry			
8	Chavandi Kalan (Aggarwal 1971: 121–123, 1978)	Many give dowry but trend is toward bridewealth	Bride's		
9	Khalapur (Hitchcock 1956:174–176, 223, 242; Hitchcock and Minturn 1966:29, 58)	Dowry preferred and most common; some cases of both at same wedding	Bride's		

10	Shoron (Pradhan 1966: 83–84)	Jats usually give dowry but there is some "buying of wives"			
11	Bunkipur (Marshall 1972:66–67, 103–105)	Thakurs give dowry; bridewealth or exchange marriages among Gardariyas	Bride's except among Gardariyas, where groom's family pays more	Chamars give dowry; poor Gardariyas give bridewealth	
12	Karimpur (Wadley and Derr 1978)	Dowry	Bride's	Dowry; occasionally poor Brahmans give bridewealth	
13	Mohana (Majumdar 1958:197)	Dowry			
14	Sherupur (Gould 1959: 221)	Dowry becoming common to all		Dowry	
15	Senapur and Madhopur (Cohn 1972:75; Luschinsky 1962: 269–271; Planalp 1956:445, 559–560)	Dowry	Bride's, but difference often slight	Both dowry and bridewealth at same wedding	Equal or groom's
16	Sadri (Chauhan 1967: 68–69, 77, 124)	Rajputs give dowry; Jats and Gadris give bridewealth; all often practice exchange marriages			
17	Awan (Gupta 1974:75–76)	Dowry	Bride's	Both dowry and bridewealth at same wedding	Bride's, but difference not great
18	Charotar villages (Pocock 1976:93, 105, 111)	Dowry		Dowry	
19	Samiala (Fukutake et al. 1964:144)	Bridewealth			

Table 9—continued

		Propertied groups		Unpropertied groups	
Index no.[a]	Site and source	Type of marriage payment	Family bearing greater costs	Type of marriage payment	Family bearing greater costs
20	Rajpur (M.S. Univ. of Baroda 1970:16)	Recent trend toward dowry		Bridewealth	
21	Nokrigram and Saragram (Veen 1976:36–56)	80% dowry, 20% exchange	Bride's	Poorest Brahmans give bridewealth	
22	Ramkheri (Mayer 1970:231–235)	Dowry, but some families accept bridewealthlike payment	Equal or groom's		
23	Nimkhera (Jacobson 1970:354)	Dowry			
24	Sasaholi (Babb 1969:87)	Dowry			
25	Bharko (Shukla 1976:149)	Dowry			
26	Supar (Fukutake et al. 1965:144)	Dowry	Bride's		Groom's among Santals
27	Kanchanpur (Basu 1962:97, 102)	Dowry			
29	Gaon (Orenstein 1965:50)	Mainly dowry; bridewealth if male highly undesirable or female desirable		Harijans give bridewealth	
31	Gopalpur (Beals 1974:104–105)	Dowry		Bridewealth	
32	Shamirpet (Dube 1967:119)	Dowry, but exchange marriages possible			

#	Location			
33	Konduru (Hiebert 1971:98)			Laborers give bridewealth[b]
34	Six villages (Reid 1978)	Dowry	Bride's	
35	Totagadde (Harper 1957:184; Wiltse Harper 1971:87)	Divaru give bridewealth		Holeru give bridewealth
36	Three villages (Claus 1970:77, 130, 276–277, 286)	Dowry		
37	Chinnapura (Regelson 1972:149)	Dowry		Bridewealth
38	Rampura (Srinivas 1976:116)	Dowrylike gifts		
41	Olappalaiyam (Beck 1972:236–237)	Dowry matched by bridewealth	Equal	
42	Nadupatti (Burkhart 1969:220)	Bridewealth, never dowry	Groom's	
44	MM (Mencher 1970: 214, 217)	Brahmans give dowry;[b] Nayaker give bridewealth		
45	Thaiyur (Djurfeldt and Lindberg 1975:237)	Rich Harijans give dowry		Poor Harijans give bridewealth or nothing
46	Endavur (Moffatt 1978)	Reddiyar give dowry		Harijans give bridewealth
47	Parangudi (Moffatt 1978)	Kallar give dowry		Harijans give bridewealth
49	Thyagasamuthiram (Silvertsen 1963: 95–99)	Dowry, but many bridewealthlike gifts from groom's side in non-Brahman weddings	Equal or groom's[b]	

143

Table 9—continued

Index no.[a]	Site and source	Propertied groups		Unpropertied groups	
		Type of marriage payment	Family bearing greater costs	Type of marriage payment	Family bearing greater costs
50	Kumbapettai (Gough 1956:834–845)	Dowry and "bridegroom wealth"		Bridewealth	
51	Tengalapatti (Dumont 1957a:30)	Bridewealth and dowry	Equal[b]		
52	Village near Melur (Dumont 1957a:30)	Gifts resembling dowry			
53	Paganeri (Dumont 1957a:30)	Gifts resembling dowry			
54	Mudukkaluttur (Dumont 1957a:31)	Bridewealth returned doubled or tripled as dowry	Bride's or equal[b]		
55	Villages near Srivaikuntham (Dumont 1957a:30)	Dowry; no bridewealth	Bride's		
56	Ramankara (Fuller 1976:67)	Dowry as gift to bride			
57	Several villages (Aiyappan 1937:56)	Nayadi give bridewealth			
58	Two fishing villages (Klausen 1968: 67–68)	Dowry		Dowry	

[a] Index numbers denote those sites of ethnographic research referred to in Table 1 and mapped in Figure 2.
[b] My interpretation.

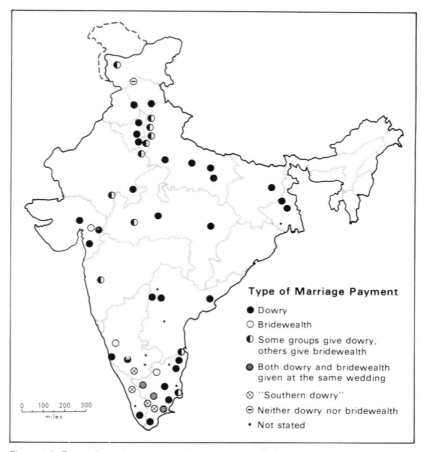

Figure 16 Type of marriage payment among propertied groups, rural India. For information on sites, see Table 9.

It is clear that dowry is widespread throughout the subcontinent; no region is completely free of this practice. Like dowry, the giving of bridewealth appears in both the North and the South. Its absence in the eastern part of India may simply be due to inadequacies in the data base. Beneath these broad generalizations, however, some interesting patterns emerge.

First, there are several cases in the North of dowry being given in the same village as bridewealth, but only one such instance of this in the South. This difference may be partially the result of the fact that in the North villages are usually multicaste and thus a wide variety of practices are more plausible. In the South single-caste villages are common. But there is another explanation that is also relevant—in northern villages there is a wider dispersal of property control throughout the population. Thus in the North there are more propertied groups in most villages than in the South.

Even more significant than intravillage variations are the differences in bridewealth and dowry between the North and the South, especially those concerning how and by whom each is given. In the North bridewealth is rarely the preferred and consistently given form of marriage payment, and it never is among the very wealthiest groups. When bridewealth is given it is usually as a last resort in order to secure a wife for a man of dubious wealth or health who is unable to "attract" a dowry-bringing bride. The sample provides two exceptions to this: the Meos (of Chavandi Kalan) and the Gardariyas (of Bunkipur). While many of the Meos continue to give large dowries as was the former custom, many have begun to adopt the giving of large amounts of bridewealth in the process of rejecting the last remnants of Hindu ways still pervading their supposedly Muslim lifestyle. The Gardariyas are an interesting case of a caste composed of families of various degrees of wealth who all give bridewealth. Every other caste in the village gives dowry.

Obviously the North is not a region monolithically characterized by dowry, for bridewealth is sometimes the custom and is at other times resorted to in case of "emergency." Bridewealth in the South is much more widespread. There the very wealthiest members of the community often openly and proudly give bridewealth. This phenomenon is more often the case when Brahmans are not to an important degree present in the village. For example, in the village of MM the Brahmans, who are generally the wealthiest people, give dowries (Mencher 1970). The Nayaker give bridewealth. Rather than being an "emergency measure," bridewealth is the accepted form which all follow. A father who gives bridewealth for his son's wedding will also accept it for his daughter's marriage.

Turning now to dowry, we find there are also North-South contrasts of note. In the North, a dowry wedding implies that the bride's side are the givers and the groom's the receivers. There is very little reciprocity between the two sides; in fact, the less the groom's side gives, the "better" the wedding. In the South where dowry is given, reciprocity between the two sides is characteristic. The only examples of this "mixed" reciprocal form are found in the South. This type of marriage is worth examining more closely.

Beck reports this kind of reciprocal transaction as being common in the Konku region of Tamil Nadu (1972:236–237). Among the Kavuntar, a peasant group, a "dowry" which may include gold, utensils, and clothing is given to the bride by her family at her marriage. This gift is "matched" by the contribution of a gold necklace and *paricam*, gifts (generally cash) given to the bride's family by the groom's. Expenses on both sides are about equal. A variation on this theme of reciprocity is found among the Brahmans of the area though they emphasize the dowry side of the exchange and de-emphasize the paricam. The dowry often includes a lump sum of cash in addition to the usual goods.

The other two cases of this kind of dowry-bridewealth exchange both come from Dumont's report on several villages and groups in the extreme South (1957a).[7] The two cases are the Pramalai Kallar and the Maravar. Among both groups a series of gifts, *cīr*, is given by the groom's side to the bride's family who "return" it either doubled (the Pramalai Kallar) or tripled (the Maravar) in jewels for the bride—a gift which may be roughly termed "dowry."

These three examples of Southern dowry differ distinctly from the northern pattern of dowry-giving in which reciprocity is minimal.[8] They can be visualized as a central point on a continuum with the situations of pure dowry and bridewealth on either extreme. In the North a major portion of what is given by the bride's parents goes to the groom's family, who may use it in turn to provide for the dowry of one of their daughters. In the South dowry more closely approximates the true meaning of stridhan, wealth given to a female which

7. Unfortunately the essay is brief. There is little in the way of background on most of the groups discussed and details on marriage transactions are scant. My interpretation of Dumont is therefore open to question.

8. In the North the groom's side usually gives a set of clothes and jewelry to the bride. This is minimal compared with what the bride's family gives.

remains in her possession and under her control in spite of marriage and which is hers to pass on to her daughters at their marriage. Dowry in the South differs also in meaning from that in the North. In the North dowry is used as a vehicle to secure a husband from a good family in order to shed glory upon the bride-givers. In the South dowry is more a gift to the bride for her own welfare and protection.

Marriage payments among unpropertied groups present a different pattern from that of the propertied groups (Table 9). It is unfortunate that there are so few cases and that the reports available are not as detailed as those on marriage payments among upper castes. Nevertheless a contrast is apparent between the reports from the northern Gangetic plain and those from the South and West. In the North, dowry—or a combination of dowry and bridewealth—is predominant. Almost all other cases throughout India are instances of bridewealth; the only exception is that of the Araya fishermen of the Kerala coast studied by Klausen.[9] Thus there does appear to be a North-South contrast in marriage payments among poorer groups (Fig. 17).

Another indicator of how the claim of sons as compared with daughters on family wealth differs throughout India is that of combined costs to either the bride's or groom's side for the marriage of an offspring. Expectations here are that overall marriage costs will be higher for the bride's side in the North in correspondence with the higher sex ratios found there. Data from the ethnographies concerning propertied groups are gathered together in Table 9. In the Gangetic plains area of the North, marriage expenses are higher for the bride's side than for the groom's. The only exception is that of the Gardariyas of Bunkipur who are bridewealth-givers. The Gaddis of Goshen village in the hills again have a contrasting pattern to that found in the plains. Although there is neither dowry nor bridewealth among the Gaddis, Newell (1978) took other costs into account to

---

9. Kerala, an area where matrilineal tendencies are strong, is also a region where dowry is the predominant form of marriage payment, among both propertied and unpropertied groups. I have discovered no case of a group with strong matrilineal tendencies who also give bridewealth. This is an important point because dowry is usually tied up with patrilinealism. But the dowry of Kerala seems quite different from dowry in northern India—in form, destination, and meaning.

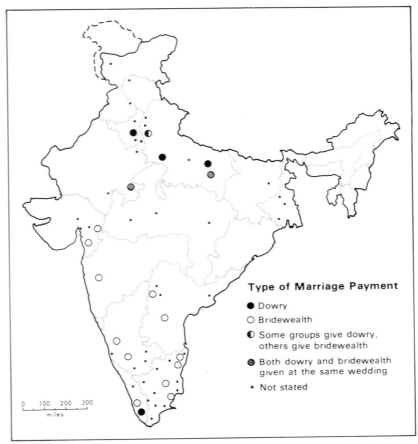

Figure 17 Type of marriage payment among unpropertied groups. rural India. For information on sites. see Table 9.

derive the conclusion that the groom's side bears the heavier overall expense of a marriage.

Traveling south from the Gangetic plain toward the central Deccan area, a case of equal expenses on both sides appears in the village of Ramkheri in Madhya Pradesh. Although dowry is the predominant form of marriage payment, when all the costs of a marriage are considered, both sides contribute almost equal amounts. Mayer notes that if there is any discrepancy, it is in the direction of heavier expenses for the family of the groom (1970:233–234). Mayer's description of the costs for both sides is interesting as it places Ramkheri in a transitional position between the northern pattern of typically heavy burdens on the bride's side only and the southern pattern of either reciprocity or greater costs for the groom's side:

> In a girl's marriage the largest outlay is for feeding and entertaining the kin and the groom's retinue. Besides this, there is the dowry and the clothes for the relatives of the groom. . . . The boy's expenses, on the other hand start with the ornaments given at the engagement, and continue with annual gifts of clothes during the engagement period. There are additional clothes to be given to the bride at the wedding, as well as the entertainment of kinsfolk before the *barat* sets off. . . . Besides, the fathers of some girls take presents of cash from the boy's parents, ostensibly to help entertainment costs. Such presents are regarded as demeaning, since the girl should be given to the groom without any thought of financial gain. But many lower caste marriages are accomplished by such transactions, and even Rajputs have married their daughters this way. In contrast to the lack of discussion about the size of the dowry (which consists only of furniture, vessels, etc., and is not inflated with jewellery [*sic*] or cash) the size of this payment is the subject of hard discussion, one might even say bargaining, by the prospective affines. [Mayer 1970:233–234]

This description bears several features in common both with the pattern of the Gangetic plain and also with many of the examples from the far South to which we shall now turn.

The six southern cases exhibit, at first, a disappointing lack of uniformity. The sheer number of cases in which the bride's side bears the heavier expenses is smaller than the number of cases in which the groom's side bears more costs. Examples of the latter are the Udaiyar of Nadupatti village and Shudra (non-Brahman) castes of Thyagasamuthiram village. The Udaiyar are a group of land owners, predominantly, who are quite unaffected by Brahmanical practices. The Shudra castes described by Sivertsen are primarily tenants, working on lands owned by Brahmans who either live in the village or are absentee landlords. The economic status of individual Shudra families varies from relative affluence to poverty. While Burkhart provides only a flat statement to the effect that the groom's side generally spends more for marriages than the bride's side, Sivertsen describes the marriage expenses in two Shudra weddings with detail. These cases are examined here with care as the author and I disagree as to which side bears the heavier costs. Here is Sivertsen's report, directly quoted, on the marriage expenses incurred by both sides in what he calls the wedding of "A":

> *Expenses met by groom's relatives:* On betrothal, presented to the girl: saris (57 Rs.), jewellery [*sic*] (165 Rs.); to the girl's mother: saris (19 Rs.).
>
> Clothes to the bridegroom (20 Rs.) and saris to his sisters (20 Rs.), and gold coins presented to the groom's mother (12 Rs.).
>
> At the wedding, dhotis presented to the following relatives of the groom: his mother's elder brother, brother's wife's brothers, sister's husbands and father's sister's husband (72 Rs.); dhotis to the following relatives of the bride: her brother, father, mother's brother, and sari to the bride's mother (76 Rs.).
>
> Other outlays: cost of invitation cards (5 Rs.); to Brahman *purohit*, Shudra *pujari*, barber, *dhobi* and musicians (18 Rs.); food, 10 units (in five bags of 120 lbs. each) of rice plus goods from the shop (150 Rs.).—*Total expenses—605 Rs.*
>
> *Expenses met by the bride's relatives:* Jewellery, brass candles, brass vessels (115 Rs.); gold ring to the bridegroom from the bride's brother (35 Rs.), *Mami Kas*, gold coins presented by the bride's mother (12 Rs.).—*Total expenses—162 Rs.*
>
> In addition, the girl's family has to give a minor feast in their village. On that occasion, however, they will receive *Moi Pannam* from the wedding guests [which will minimize, if not cover, the cost of the feast]. . . .
>
> The bride's other relatives, her mother's brothers, her sisters and mother's sisters . . . presented gold coins worth 60 Rs. to the couple. From the groom's other relatives the bride received the following gifts: From his mother's brother—gold ring, gold coin and *Tali*, the marriage thread (50 Rs.); from the groom's sister's husband—and sister's husband's brothers—gold coins (24 Rs.). There was further received in cash from the bride's affines . . . 26 Rs. which went to the groom, and from the groom's affines 10 Rs. which went to the bride. *Moi Pannam* from 109 guests amounted to 200 Rs. In total the groom received from the girl's family and her affines, and from his own relatives and other guests 614 Rs., which gives a balance of 9 Rs.

For the wedding of "B" expenses are described as follows:

> *Expenses of the groom's family:* Jewellery to the bride and groom (120 Rs.); dhotis and saris in exchange for gold rings and gold coins

(120 Rs.); to the priests, village servants and for food, etc. 95 Rs.—
Total outlay 335 Rs.

The value of the bride's dowry is 115 Rs. From relatives gold worth
145 Rs. was received and *Moi Pannam* from 50 guests totalled 116
Rs. In total, 376 Rs. was received, which gives a balance over direct
outlays of 41 Rs.

It can be seen from the examples given here that among non-
Brahmins as among Brahmins, the cost of marrying daughters is higher than that of marrying sons. [Sivertsen 1963:97–99]

Working with the information which Sivertsen provides for both
marriages, I have reached a rather different conclusion: at least in the
two marriages described, it can be more expensive to marry a son
than a daughter, or expenses can be approximately equal for both.
Sivertsen's conclusion appears to be based more on his assessment of
how much the groom "nets" rather than a direct comparison of costs
to either side, regardless of the destination of the gifts. My analysis,
which rearranges some of Sivertsen's data concerning the expenses of
affines, is as follows for the wedding of "A":

Expenses to the groom's side:

saris	Rs. 57
jewelry	165
saris	10
clothes	20
saris	20
gold coins	12
dhotis	72
dhotis and sari	76
invitations	5
priest, etc.	18
food	150
gold ring, gold coin, tali	50
gold coins	24
cash	10
Total	689

Expenses to the bride's side:

jewelry and brass items	115
gold ring	35
gold coins	12
gold coins	60
cash	26
Total	248

It is quite obvious that the groom's side is responsible for a significantly larger outlay of funds (Rs. 689) than the bride's (Rs. 248). There is no way that a contrary conclusion can be reached. Similarly, the wedding expense for the marriage of "B" can be reconstructed as follows:

Expenses to the groom's side:

jewelry	120
dhotis, saris	120
fee for priest, servants, food	95
Total	335

Expenses to the bride's side:

dowry	115
gold rings and coins	120
gold	145
Total	380

In the case of this latter wedding, costs to the bride's side are only slightly higher than those borne by the groom's side. Furthermore, the bride's side receives the *moi pannam* contributions from the guests (Rs. 116) which offset their costs greatly. Therefore I have taken the liberty of contradicting the author's statement and assigned the heavier burden to the groom's side for non-Brahman groups of Thyagasamuthiram village.

As shown in the preceding examples, reciprocity between the two sides characterizes the entire chain of marriage expenses in the South. Such reciprocity has been discussed by Dumont (1957a:30–31) in his report on marriage expenses among the Pramalai Kallar of western Madurai District, Tamil Nadu, and of other Kallar groups in the southern reaches of the state. Although Dumont feels that, on the whole, the bride's side pays more in all of these groups, I conclude from my reading of his and other reports that the difference may be only very slight, if there is any difference at all. According to Dumont, the paricam is returned doubled in the form of jewelry; gifts exchanged at the wedding ceremony are of equal cost for both sides. It can be only carelessness which translates this series of exchanges into a situation of greater expense for the bride's side. Let me explain. Assume that the paricam given by the groom's family is worth

Rs. 100; then the value of the jewelry which the bride's family gives is Rs. 200. Gifts given at the ceremony are of equal worth so they cancel each other out. But it cannot be said that, since the bride's family gives Rs. 200 of jewelry, they spent Rs. 200 of their own money. In actuality they spent only Rs. 100, just as the groom's side did, but they used at the same time the groom's side's contribution of Rs. 100 to augment their own donation. This rethinking of Dumont's report indicates a very clear case of reciprocity.

Such clear reciprocity is not the case among the two remaining southern cases: the Maravar of Mudukkulattur village and the Nangudi Vellalar of several villages in Tirunelveli District. Dumont states that among the Maravar, gifts from the groom's side are returned tripled by the bride's side (1957a:31). This means that the bride's side contributes twice as much, excluding the portion received from the groom's side. Nevertheless there is more marked reciprocity than in the North. The second case is very intriguing. Here is an example, in the far South of India, of marriage payments of which the outward features resemble the northern dowry pattern—great amounts of money being spent on the bride's side and minimal returns from the groom's side (for among the Nangudi Vellalar, the contribution from the groom's side in fact is very slight). There is no paricam, no tali, no gift of saris. While the cost of various feasts is shared equally by both sides, all other expenses, including the dowry, are borne by the family of the bride. I assume, however, that all these costs still come nowhere near the huge amounts spent on a northern Jat wedding.

The regional pattern of overall marriage costs is one of general North-South contrast. In the northern Gangetic plains region expenses are clearly greater on the bride's side. In the central region there is an indication of a transition to greater reciprocity between both sides, a situation found in many instances in the South. However, the South exhibits internal variation such that in some cases the groom's side bears greater overall costs, in some cases costs are equal, and in some cases from the South a situation of greater costs for the bride's side reappears (very similar in form but not degree to the northern pattern).

Among unpropertied groups the pattern of overall marriage costs is quite different from that of the propertied groups, according to the few cases mentioned in the literature (Table 9). Most ethnographers state that heavier costs are borne by the groom's side, or that costs are fairly equal. Only one of the five cases notes that the bride's side pays more, although the difference in costs to both sides is not great. It may be sheer coincidence that this latter case is found in the North while all the others are to the South or East, but there are too few cases to make a definitive statement.

Minimal-cost Marriages

A subject that has not attracted much attention from anthropologists writing on India is marriages involving little extravagance and expenditure. The problems inherent in trying to assess the extent of practices that are not well described in the literature can be only too apparent. Of the two types of marriage considered in this section— cousin marriage and "exchange" marriage—the former has received much more attention than the latter, perhaps because exchange marriages are often not the preferred form and people therefore may be less willing to discuss its practice or admit to its frequency.

The general rule regarding marriage costs when cousins are wed is: the more closely the bride and groom are related, the smaller the costs will be. Are such marriages distributed equally within India? The answer is no; cousin marriages are much more frequent in the South. Beck reports that in the Konku region of Tamil Nadu, marriage between real cousins occurs in 17.4 percent of all cases (1972:253). Beals tells us that the frequency of marriages between "close relatives" in Elephant is 52 percent, in Gopalpur 21 percent, and in Namhalli 33 percent (1974:115). Moffatt reports that 70 to 80 percent of all marriages among the Harijans he studied in Tamil Nadu are between classificatory cross-cousins (1978). This list could be added to at length but more examples would not change the point that marriage between close relatives is not merely the ideal in the South but also the actual practice. There is little in the way of concrete evidence on frequencies of cousin marriage in the North, though among Muslims all over India cousin marriage is preferred.

It is interesting that the regional distribution of cousin marriages is complementary to that of systematized hypergamy, a preponderantly

Northern practice. Logically, in fact, the two practices should be mutually exclusive, as one—cousin marriage—demands reciprocity of mates between two families regardless of their material and social standing, while the other—hypergamy—requires inequality between bride-givers and bride-takers. Also in terms of marriage costs, the two systems are very different. Cousin marriage reduces costs to both parties; hypergamy creates high costs for the family of the bride. It is significant that the form that makes daughters a great expense is found in the North and not the South.

The extent of the practice of exchange marriages is much more difficult to assess. The term "exchange marriage" usually refers to a marriage in which a son and a daughter in one family are married to a daughter and a son of another family; spouses are thus in fact exchanged. Sometimes, though, the term appears to be used to refer also to marriages between two sisters of one family and two brothers of another; strictly speaking spouses are not exchanged here. Wherever the practice is found, however, a reduction in costs to both sides involved usually occurs. For example, Dube notes that in Shamirpet village, near Hyderabad city in the Deccan plateau, exchange marriages are performed specifically to economize on the amount of dowry (1967:119). There is an added advantage, mentioned by the same author, in performing two weddings at one time: guests need be feasted and entertained only once, priests are paid only once, and so on.

Given the fact that the spirit of the Brahmanical ideal of *kanyādān*, or the gift of a daughter in marriage with no thought of gain, is violated by exchange marriages, because bride-givers are simultaneously bride-takers, one would guess that exchange marriages are less practiced by Brahman jatis and other high-level groups who are influenced by Brahmanical ways. In other words, one could expect that low-cost exchange marriages are more frequent among lower-level groups and in the South where Brahmanical influences are less pervasive.

Marriage Costs and Female Mortality

When Bipat's mother gave birth to a fourth son, a Thakur woman who was among the first to hear passed the word on to others. Her broad smile spoke for itself before she related the news and said, "Every time a boy is born in the village I feel very happy. The whole day I can't think of anything else. I feel just as happy as I would feel if a boy were born in my own family." This same woman looked very down-cast when a baby girl was born in her family not long afterward. Far more girls than boys had been born in her family in recent years, and the financial burden of their marriages was telling on the family re-serve. They longed for more male members of the family, but their wishes were not being fulfilled. One day this Thakur woman held her baby granddaughter up in the air and said, "Now she should die. I tell her she should die. She is growing bigger and soon there will be the problem of finding a husband for her. For the last five days, my nephew has been wandering here and there in search of grooms for Tara and Koshora. It's a great worry." Often when she thought of the consequences of another female member of the family, she spoke in this way, but always in her personal relations with the baby, she was loving and affectionate. If the baby were to die, the grandmother would be greatly affected by the loss. No one could doubt this. But a baby girl is not just a person in her own right. She is also a member of her sex group and she places upon her parents many obligations and responsibilities. [Luschinsky 1962:82]

The above quotation dramatically illustrates the major implication of this chapter: that marriage costs are an important cultural motiva-tion for strong preferences regarding the sex of children. When the payment of large dowries is both the ideal and the actual practice, many daughters are indeed a serious threat to the prosperity and strength of the family. That such a situation could motivate uncon-scious discrimination in favor of boys and against girls is very plausible.

At the outset of this chapter I suggested that the high cost of daughters' marriages is a major element in the emic perspective of the Indian peasant's attitude concerning the sex of offspring. I hypothe-sized that where dowry and overall costs of marriage for daughters are significant, the survival rates of girls will suffer. On the other hand, where such costs are either minimal or nonexistent, which is the case in much of rural India, I posited a more favorable rate of survival of girls compared with boys.

The relationships which these patterns in the costs of marriage have to juvenile sex ratios are very illuminating. In northern prop-ertied groups there is, as expected, a clear correspondence between

marriage costs and juvenile sex ratios: marriage costs are high and so
are sex ratios, indicating high female mortality where costs of marrying daughters are most prohibitive. In southern unpropertied groups
there is a fairly close correspondence: marriage costs and juvenile sex
ratios are both low or low-medium. But the situation is less clear
among the northern unpropertied and southern propertied groups. In
the southern propertied groups, although marriage costs for the
bride's family range from low to high, juvenile sex ratios are never
high. In northern unpropertied groups, while marriage costs tend to
be low, sex ratios are moderately high. This situation is relevant to
that discovered when the relationship between female labor participation and juvenile sex ratios was studied. In the North there is again
less preservation of female life than what marriage costs predict,
while in the South we find greater preservation of female life than
what marriage costs would predict. The chart below presents the
findings for the three factors of female labor participation, marriage
costs, and juvenile sex ratios:

Category	Female labor participation	Marriage costs	Juvenile sex ratios
Northern propertied	Low	High	High
Southern propertied	Low-medium-high	Low-medium-high	Low
Northern unpropertied	High	Low	Medium
Southern unpropertied	High	Low	Low-medium

A fascinating picture of the interrelationships between the labor
participation rates of females, pattern of marriage costs, and juvenile sex ratios is revealed here. FLP rates and marriage costs are
perfectly correspondent, inversely. When FLP rates are high, marriage costs are low and vice versa. Thus the etic view of what determines female worth in rural India matches the emic view, even
though each is based on different factors. One could say the emic
view is a translation of the etic situation into the metaphor of marriage costs.

Unfortunately both female labor participation rates and marriage
costs fail to account completely for variation in juvenile sex ratios.
While both these factors are obviously related in a strong way to sex
ratios in rural India, they do not provide the total explanation. They

do explain sex ratios for the northern propertied groups and the southern unpropertied groups but they do not do so completely for the northern unpropertied groups and the southern propertied groups. The reason can be only guessed at for now.

This guess revolves around the theory that there are two main cultural cores in India, the Brahmanical (of the Northwest) and the Dravidian or the Agamic (of the South). The Brahmanic system is in the process of spreading while the Dravidian is retrenching. Exactly why this is so is an interesting problem in itself. Further, Brahmanism is most solidly established among the upper social strata of northern India. As a model for change Brahmanism is most emulated by the northern lower social strata, that is, by the people "nearest" to where it is firmly situated. Agricultural economy, physical distance and topographical barriers, and extant cultural practices in the South are all important impediments to Brahmanism's expansion there. However, inroads are being made, first among the propertied class, the females of which are beginning more and more to be removed from an active role in agricultural production and increasingly to emphasize dowry over reciprocity or bridewealth. Least affected by Brahmanical ways are the southern unpropertied groups; they are socially most distinct and physically most distant from the core of Brahmanism. In this way the two categories with those juvenile sex ratios not fully explained by either female labor participation rates or marriage costs—the northern unpropertied and the southern propertied—can be seen as the two categories most in flux between Brahmanical and Dravidian lifestyles. It is, however, likely that the superficial copying of certain northern features in the South will not easily displace the deeply institutionalized behavior there that fosters female survival.

8
Son Preference
and "Family Planning"

In rural India the most important benefits that derive from having many sons have been compiled by May and Heer in their classic study of son survivorship (1968); I will largely follow their categorization of the values of sons: (1) the transmission of family property and name, (2) economic support for the parents when they grow old or in case of earlier disability, (3) performance of the ancestral (*śrāddha*) rites for the father after his death to ensure the peace of his soul, and (4) financial interests since a family must provide a dowry for the marriage of a daughter while no payment is necessary for a son's marriage and since there is the added advantage of bringing in a bride with *her* dowry.[1] I suggest that these reasons for preferring sons to daughters do not apply with equal force to different geographical regions within India or to all social strata.

Inheritance. The first reason for wanting sons is to have someone to inherit the family property and name. Considering only property here (for the notion of "family name" can be equated with property in most cases), it is obvious that sons could be of little value as heirs to a family having little or no property. Since land is the major form of

1. I have altered the list presented by May and Heer in only one way, that is, by collapsing the separate categories of "economic support" and "emotional support" into one category since each is influenced by the same factor, namely, the son staying with the parents in their old age.

property in rural India, we can refer to the proportions of landed and landless people in order to assess the extent of this aspect of the desire for sons.

For rural India as a whole, the class of owner-cultivators comprises about 50 percent of the total economically active male population.[2] Thus half the rural population is relatively less in need of a son than the other half. Regional differences in the proportion of landed to landless people are important here: landholders are found in greater percentages in the northern area of India than in the South. For example, in the northern state of Uttar Pradesh (1951) the land-owning cultivators comprised more than three-quarters of the rural population. The percentage of landholders is lower in the southern section of the country. In much of Kerala, Andhra Pradesh, Karnata-ka, and Tamil Nadu, the percentage of landless laborers exceeded 30 percent of the agricultural classes. Generalizing from data available, it can be said that the North has roughly seven property-holders to every four in the South. Logically, then, the desire for sons as heirs (that is, of the ancestral property) should be much more widespread throughout the population in the North.

Further, while sons may be the preferred heirs in both North and South India, daughters are often accepted as heirs in the South—though rarely are they in the North. In several ethnographic reports on South Indian villages, authors mention that a daughter may inherit rights to land at partition or a daughter may in her dowry be given rights to land, rights that actually pass from her natal family's hands to those of the newly married couple (Reid 1978; Montgomery 1972:71; Dumont 1957*b*:201; Fuller 1976:66; Klausen 1968:68). All the cases are from the far South.

Another indication that daughters are more often heirs in the South comes from reading the ethnographic reports on *gharjamāī* mar-riages, those in which the son-in-law comes to live with the bride and her natal family. Although gharjamai marriages take place all over India, the frequency with which they occur in the South seems to be

2. These and the following figures are from the 1951 Census of India and were provided by Sopher from his personal notes for which I am grateful. Although there may have been some changes due to land reform since 1951, the general pattern is still relevant to the discussion here and to the 1961 data on sex ratios.

greater. Unfortunately I have no hard evidence to substantiate this impression; an investigation of the subject would be very valuable.

Support in old age. Another reason for wanting sons is that they provide for their parents' economic support in old age and in case of earlier disability. Indian peasants are often quoted as saying that sons are preferred over daughters because they stay with the family forever, but girls grow up merely to leave the home and join another family. The validity of such folk sayings also varies with region and social level.

Marriage is the most important factor affecting the ability of daughters to support their parents. The well-known custom of female seclusion, purdah, in North India seems only superficially important here. While purdah does seriously curtail the economic activities of married women when in their husband's village, it has little impact on the female's economic role in her natal village for "daughters of the village" typically observe very few restrictions, if any at all.[3]

Social and regional differences in the degree to which a daughter is separated by marriage from her natal home can be summarized briefly. Among higher social groups there is generally a greater distance between the bride's natal village and her village of marriage,[4] higher frequency of village exogamous marriages,[5] and lower frequency and

3. Jacobson describes a case of a group of Rajputs in a village near Nimkhera in which daughters observe purdah restrictions in their natal village (1970:157). This is a rare instance. The same author in a different place contrasts the freedom of girls in their natal villages with the restrictions imposed on them in the homes and villages of their affines (1972:7).

4. Gould (1960) and Mayer (1970) both assert that higher-status groups generally marry their daughters at farther distances than do lower-status groups. Their conclusions have been questioned by Freed and Freed (1973) and Mahar (1966). The latter insists that the relationship between status and the spatial range of marriages is not so simple. Mahar emphasizes the particular patterns of each caste or status level in the village where he studied and shies away from making any overall generalizations. He did find, however, that the dominant caste in the village, the Rajputs (who are 42 percent of the population and own 90 percent of the land), have by far the longest marriage distances. While individual patterns for less numerous and less powerful castes are interesting, the important point should not escape the reader that dominant groups usually have the most far-reaching affinal ties.

5. Mayer (1970:209) states that village endogamy is practiced only by those

shorter duration of visits to the natal village.[6] Among groups of lower status, marriage distance tends to be shorter, there is lower frequency in the practice of village exogamy, and the married woman is often free to walk the distance from her husband's village to her natal village by herself.

Recent research has also exposed broad regional variations in the degree to which a daughter is separated from, or retains close ties with, her natal family. Generally in the North, marriage distances are much greater than in the South (Libbee and Sopher 1975; Libbee 1980). In the North, also, village exogamy is practiced to a much greater degree than it is in the South. We can conclude that the chances of a bride visiting her natal village, if indeed she does not live there already, are better in the South than in the North, where distance may provide a significant barrier.

Ritual. Leaving behind the subject of the economic importance of sons versus daughters, let us turn to an area in which the role of the son could not possibly be filled by a daughter—that of religion. The necessity of having a son to perform the ancestral (sraddha) rites for the father after his death is constantly reiterated in the literature. Females are not allowed, by religious law, to perform any Vedic rituals; a daughter is useless when it comes to keeping the dead at peace.

Basic knowledge of Hinduism and Indian social structure indicates that there must be social and regional variations in the significance of this reason for desiring sons. Although I am sure that the ancestral rites are not practiced by all social groups, it is difficult to assess the

---

people "too poor to find wives elsewhere." Madan (1965:112) notes that although village exogamy is preferred, village endogamy does occur. He does not say whether there are more village endogamous marriages among lower social groups, but the fact that such are "undesirable" probably means that they are resorted to only by less wealthy families. Veen (1972:81–82) associates marriages within the village with poverty. These are all northern sources.

6. Jacobson (1972:9–10) writes that in Nimkhera, visits of upper-class women to their natal homes may be longer in duration than those of lower-class women, while Luschinsky (1962:349–350) states that in Senapur, visits of upper-class women are shorter. Reports from the South make no distinctions in visiting pattern between upper and lower social strata.

actual distribution of the phenomenon. Ethnographic data on this subject are sparse. One could very arbitrarily say that members of all twice-born castes perform the rite and therefore require sons for this purpose, whereas Shudras and untouchables would not need sons for this reason because they do not perform the Vedic rite. Yet the validity of this statement could be questioned. One possible way of assessing the regional variation of the need for sons for ritual performance is to take the percentage of Brahmans in the population as an indicator of the extent to which any Brahmanical ritual would be practiced. The percentage of Brahmans in the total population is much higher in the North than in the South (Schwartzberg 1978). Although generalizations on this matter are tentative, it seems probable that ancestral rites are practiced most frequently in northern India among the higher social strata.

Financial aspects. The last major benefit of having sons which needs to be considered is that sons are not as expensive to marry off as daughters, whose marriages require dowries. The marriage of a son is, in fact, supposedly financially advantageous to a family, as his bride brings wealth with her in the form of her dowry. Since the subject of marriage expenses was fully discussed in Chapter 7, I will here simply give a brief summary of the relevant findings.

Families of the upper social level in the North are the major segment of the population affected by the expense of paying for a large dowry for a daughter's wedding and also by the advantage of having sons whose brides will bring in large dowries. In most other groups either the size of the dowry is minimal, often not involving cash payments at all, or else bridewealth is the rule. Obviously in the latter case it is a financial advantage to have a daughter and not a son.

From this assessment of the varying degree of the desire for sons among rural Indians, it is apparent that there are striking differences, both regional and social, which must be taken into account. In order to visualize these variations in the need for sons, the information is displayed below:

Class	Reason for son preference	Degree of son preference in North	Degree of son preference in South
Propertied	Inheritance	Intense	Moderate
	Support	Intense	Moderate
	Ritual	Intense	Moderate
	Dowry	Intense	—
Unpropertied	Inheritance	—	—
	Support	Moderate	Moderate
	Ritual	—	—
	Dowry	Moderate	—

Northern upper-status groups rank highest in the need for sons. In fact, they are the only category with "intense" ratings. Southern upper-status groups and northern lower-status groups are almost equal in their need for sons, while southern lower-status groups have the least need for sons.

Sons and Population Growth

Are there major differences in population increase according to socioeconomic status and region in rural India which correspond to the variations in the degree to which sons are desired?[7] If there is a causal relationship between the desire for sons and population growth in rural India, then we should find the highest rates of increase in the North, especially among the upper social strata there. Lower rates of population growth should characterize the South and the lower social groups.

There are many ways to measure population growth and fertility (percentage of annual rate of growth, number of live births per year, and so on). For none of these are there dependable data for India,

7. Authors stressing the importance of the desire for sons in affecting the size of Indian families or as being a major barrier to the success of family-planning programs in India are Agarwala (1964), Davies (1976), Mamdani (1972), Mandelbaum (1974), May and Heer (1968), Pathare (1966), Poffenberger (1968), Taylor (1969), Wyon and Gordon (1971). Williamson (1978) in her excellent review article refers to it as "the son barrier." McClelland (1979) discusses methods used to assess the effect of sex preferences on fertility; unfortunately he fails to consider the fertility-depressing potential of daughter neglect.

particularly for each rural district and over time. There have been
some local surveys performed: the Mysore study (U.N. 1961) and the
Singur study in West Bengal (Mathen 1962) are two famous ones, but
these isolated studies do not allow the formation of the sort of broad
regional picture which is needed to compare with the patterns of son
preference and daughter discrimination sketched above. The scant
and undependable evidence that does exist is aggregated by state. The
Sample Registration Bulletin of India provides fertility data (fertility
is defined as the number of live births per woman over her entire
reproductive period) for 1971–1972 (quoted in Gulhati 1978). According to this survey, Gujarat, Madhya Pradesh, Uttar Pradesh,
Rajasthan, and Bihar all have much higher fertility rates than the other
states included in the survey (no data were available on the Punjab).
These data may indicate that the North has a higher birth rate than the
South, consistent with the "son preference boosts fertility" hypothesis. But when we consider a different measure of population
growth—the decennial growth rates of the total population by state—
quite similar figures are found for both northern and southern states
(India 1972:20–21).

Admittedly the above data leave much to be desired, but the broad
patterns they present do make a certain amount of sense. First, because of extreme son preference in the North, the birth rate is high as
families attempt to maximize the number of sons. However, as a
result of the fatal neglect of daughters, that high birth rate is to some
extent mitigated—just how much can only be inferred since the decennial growth rates are affected by both mortality and migration. It
is clear, though, that a measure of Indian population growth cannot
consider merely the number of live births since a significant number
of those born do not live to reproduce, particularly North Indian
females.

A far more accurate measure would be the gross reproduction rate:
"the average number of daughters that would be borne by a cohort of
females all of whom lived to the end of the childbearing period if the
cohort bore children according to a given set of age-specific fertility
rates" (U.N. 1977:101 n. 4). In other words, it is the number of
females who survive to reproduce other females who also survive to
reproduce which is critical in influencing the rate of population

growth. The importance of unbalanced sex ratios (in favor of males) has been addressed by Kelly (1975:179–181), who finds that sex differences in infant mortality in the Punjab "are responsible for a 'saving' in population growth of 7.78%" of what the population would have been in the projected year 2040. If it were not for the effects of daughter neglect, population growth spurred by the desire for sons would have been greater. Obviously daughter neglect does not completely wipe out the fertility-boosting effect of son prefer- ence, but it does temper it.[8]

While examining the relationship between social class and fertility, I uncovered the very serious problem that few of the numerous analy- ses of socioeconomic differentials in fertility have been consistent in their use of criteria for defining class or status or, for that matter, fertility. Some studies have simply equated class with caste, or with income, or with expenditures, or with the size of landholdings. For assessing fertility rates, some scholars have employed the number of births per 1,000 women per year, some the number of children under the age of five years per 1,000 women, some the number of children under the age of five years per 1,000 ever-married women or currently married women or currently married women between the ages of fifteen and forty-four or fifteen and forty-five. Given this bewildering array of criteria and categories, it is not sur- prising that it is so difficult to form any generalizations about popula- tion increase and social class which are not contradictable on the basis of one study or another. Perhaps the safest statement that can be made is that there appears to be a tendency for lower-level groups to have higher birth rates than higher-level groups. But, due to higher infant mortality among the former, actual completed family size does not differ significantly from one level to the other.

Let us narrow the perspective now to examine the case of a more defined group, the group that should have the highest growth in all India if there is a clear causal relationship between the desire for sons and high rates of population increase: the "caste" of Brahmans. Brah- mans rank very high on the scale of son-desiring groups; for each of

8. A very important research topic lies in the expansion of the boundaries of my study through comparison of Western Asia with Southeast Asia in terms of cultural treatment of women, sex ratios, and population dynamics.

the four reasons presented above, most Brahman families should intensely desire sons. But do Brahmans consistently have larger families than other groups? 1931 Census figures show that Brahmans have smaller child-woman ratios than other castes and, although the size difference may not be statistically significant, it is clear that Brahman families are not *larger* than others. The probability that Brahmans have a lower gross reproductive rate than other groups is supported by the fact that the proportion of Brahmans in the Indian population shrank in the first half of the twentieth century.[9]

Females in Danger

The moral issues and policy questions raised by these findings are complex and their complexity is compounded by current events. There is some indication that the proportion of females in India is on the decline (Dandekar 1975), particularly in West Bengal. This suggestion needs to be fully investigated in order to assess whether the juvenile population is also experiencing a higher sex ratio, and if so where and why. Then the Indian government must decide if it wants to take steps to try to reverse the situation, perhaps following the example of mainland China, and educating people away from son preference (Williamson 1978). Certainly development efforts that detract from female employment should be carefully examined to see what their impact will be on female labor participation and female domestic status.

The future of females in India is also jeopardized by increasing possibilities of sex selection of offspring at the time of conception. If such a choice were ever made widely available to the Indian population, there is no doubt that people would opt for many more sons than daughters, particularly in the North. True, this would have the highly beneficial effect of reducing the number of unwanted daughters born and thus of reducing their suffering and wastage through neglect and

9. Davis (1946:247) writes that "the Brahmans . . . have long been regarded as less fertile than the rest of the population; indeed, they have steadily diminished as a proportion of the total Hindu population despite an infiltration from other castes. . . ."

discrimination. However, it could well return the sex ratio of the population to its pre-twentieth-century configuration—there might again be entire villages without a single daughter. Sex control at conception shares with female infanticide a great degree of "efficiency" in increasing the maleness of the population—efficient in the sense that male offspring are obtained and female offspring tidily avoided. However, such "efficiency" certainly has its dangers. Unless a concerted effort is made soon to counteract the forces promoting son preference, unless the victimization of North Indian daughters is slowed, then cultural sway will prevail, demanding the demise of fertility, of childbearing, of the female.

Appendix A
Sex Ratios at Birth in India

The possibility has been raised periodically that higher proportions of males to females in the Indian population are the result of imbalances that occur at the time of birth. Generally the data employed to support this theory are census reports and people's memory of the sex of children born to them. The only completely dependable data on sex ratio at birth come from records of large numbers of births that have occurred in hospitals.

One very important study has been done which should banish forever suspicions that sex ratios at birth vary by region and could thus explain the regional pattern of high masculinity in the North: Ramachandran and Deshpande's analysis of thousands of hospital births that occurred throughout India (1964). The authors found the following sex ratios for live births (the number of births recorded in each zone exceeds 100,000): North zone 104, East zone 106, South zone 106, West zone 107, Central zone 108, and the Northwest zone 107. These findings clearly show that sex ratio at birth cannot be the explanation for the very high juvenile sex ratios found in North India, for according to these hospital births, the range of sex ratio at birth is from 104 to 108 with the lowest in what is called the North zone! Another author discovered an average sex ratio at birth of 104 for over 20,000 births in Calcutta's Chetla Health Centre (Goon 1975). This report of hospital births in Calcutta is interesting when juxtaposed to sex ratio at birth reported *from memory* by a group of industrial laborers interviewed in Calcutta (Mathew 1947). Of the 1,848 children reported to have been born the sex ratio was 120. Mathew attributes this very high ratio to the fact that the sample may be biased by the inclusion of many incomplete families, since it has been hypothesized that sex ratios are higher among earlier-born children. True, studies have shown that lower parity births have slightly higher sex ratios than higher parity births but the difference is not great enough to effect a sex ratio as high as 120. Rather, the sex ratio Mathew obtained from his informants' memories is the result of cultural skewing—daughters who were born (and may have died) have been forgotten. Sons are rarely forgotten.

Confirmation that sex ratios at birth throughout India consistently fall within the range of normality is confirmed also by a careful analysis of National Sample Survey data performed by Pakrasi and Halder (1971). They found that Indian sex ratios at birth are similar to those of Europe, except for a greater preponderance of males in first births. Again, these are reported data and are subject to cultural skewing which is probably the cause of the apparent high masculinity among first-born offspring. Let us now turn to a brief examination of the facts behind such "cultural skewing."

Cultural preferences for children of either sex can affect the accuracy of census data; Rukanuddin has proposed this possibility in terms of Pakistani census data (1967). In the northern part of India there are two obvious factors at work which could result in the under-reporting of female births. (These factors may also be present in South India but to a much smaller extent.) The act of giving birth is always shrouded from the public and tightly controlled by the immediate family. Both factors—the distance from the bride's natal village and the traditional system of announcing births—arise from this situation and work together to affect census data.

In rural India it is common for the wife to go to her natal house for confinement, especially for the first delivery. Thus custom is widespread throughout at least North India but it is by no means universally held even there. In the North, the distance between the bride's natal home and her home of marriage is generally much farther than it is in the South where both houses may even be in the same village (see Chapter 8). This distance factor can have severe repercussions on the registration of female births since the birth should be registered in the mother's village of marriage, not her village of birth.

The way in which the news of a birth travels from one village to another is quite standard as reported in ethnographies on North Indian villages. If a son is born, there is much noisy celebrating and a messenger is speedily sent to the husband's village to spread the glad tidings. In contrast, the birth of a daughter is greeted by silence. No messenger is immediately dispatched; sometime later a postcard will be mailed notifying the husband and his family. It is almost as if nothing at all had happened. Rukanuddin is certainly correct in his observation that joy about a birth increases knowledge of that birth (1967:159). Likewise the solemn silence which greets a girl's birth decreases knowledge of that birth.

There is little doubt that both distance and the way a birth is reported can have a significant effect on the recorded sex ratio at birth (especially that of first births when it is most common for a woman to go to her natal home for her confinement). Both factors work to minimize the fact that a female has been born at all. How well such a situation also could cover up the practice of outright female infanticide can be easily imagined. Further, the existence of a daughter who was not really wanted will also never be officially recognized, so that if she were to die prematurely through neglect, her death, likewise, would go unnoticed.

Cultural preferences for sons could also affect the census records of other age groups besides neonates and infants. Vital events for females of all ages seem to be consistently underrecorded. Reports from northern villages indicate that genealogies of many generations are kept for families, but for their male members only (Leaf 1978; Lewis 1965:342–343; Hitchcock 1956:48–49; Wadley and Derr 1978). Although Kelly (1975:43) feels that underreporting of females at all ages is not necessarily the case, it is my feeling that the possibility is too strong to be dismissed. The safest generalization about birth reporting in South Asia is that if there is a recurrent pattern of misreporting or unconscious underreporting, it will be in the direction of reducing the number of female births (or deaths) registered. The rule is: those who "count" will be counted, those who don't "count" may not be.

Appendix B
1961 Census of India
Definition of Work

The definition of "work" according to the 1961 Census of India is revealed in the following excerpt from the general instructions to enumerators found in the introduction to each major volume:

"The basis of work will be satisfied in the case of seasonal work like cultivation, livestock, dairying, household industry etc., if the person has had some regular work of more than one hour a day throughout the greater part of the working season. In the case of regular employment in any trade, profession, service, business or commerce, the basis of work will be satisfied if the person was employed during any of the fifteen days preceding the day on which you visited the household. If on the check or revisional round such a person is found to be unemployed no change in the original entry should be made. A person who is working but was absent from his work during the fifteen days preceding the day on which enumerated or even exceeding the period of fifteen days due to illness or other work but has not actually joined should be treated as non-worker. . . .

"An adult woman who is engaged in household duties but doing no other productive work to augment the family's resources should not be considered as working for purposes of this question. If, however, in addition to her household work she engages herself in work such as rice pounding for sale or wages, or in domestic services for wages for others or minding cattle or selling firewood or making and selling cowdung cakes or grass etc., or any such work she should be treated as a worker."

References

Abraham, Thomas, Sujeshwar N. Saxena, and Ranjit Sen. 1969. "Bacterial and Parasitic Findings in Diarrhoea in the Young: A Study of 500 Consecutive Untreated Cases in New Delhi." *Indian Pediatrics* 6:476–482.

Adams, Kathleen J. 1972. "The Barama River Caribs of Guyana Restudied: Forty Years of Cultural Adaptation and Population Change." Unpublished doctoral dissertation, Case Western Reserve University.

——. 1976. Personal communication.

Adelman, Irma, and George Dalton. 1971. "Developing Village India: A Statistical Analysis." In George Dalton, ed., *Studies in Economic Anthropology*. Washington, D.C.: American Anthropological Association. Pp. 180–232.

Agarwala, S. N. 1964. "Social and Cultural Factors Affecting Fertility in India." *Population Review* 8(1):73–78.

Aggarwal, Partap C. 1971. *Caste, Religion and Power: An Indian Case Study*. New Delhi: Shri Ram Centre for Industrial Relations.

——. 1978. Questionnaire response.

Aginsky, B. W. 1939. "Population Control in the Shanel (Pomo) Tribe." *American Sociological Review* 4(2):209–216.

Agrawal, J. P., Shantilal C. Sheth, and N. S. Tibrewala. 1969. "Rickets—A Study of 300 Cases." *Indian Pediatrics* 6:792–800.

Ahmed, Iqbal, and J. K. G. Webb. 1963. "Childhood Diarrhoea in South India." *Indian Journal of Childhood Health* 12(2):85–91.

Aiyappan, A. 1937. *Social and Physical Anthropology of the Nayadis of Malabar*. Bulletin of the Madras Government Museum, New Series, General Section, Volume II, No. 4. Madras, India: The Superintendent, Government Press.

Akhtar, Rais. 1971. "A Note on the Nutritional Geography of Karimganj Village." *The National Geographic Journal of India* 27(4):207–214.

Anand, D., and A. Rama Rao. 1962. "Feeding Practices of Infants and Toddlers in Najafgarh Area." *Indian Journal of Child Health* 11:172–181.

Apthekar, Herbert. 1931. *Anjea: Infanticide, Abortion, and Contraception in Savage Society*. New York: William Godwin.

Ascádi, György. 1976. "Traditional Birth Control Methods in Yorubaland." In Marshall and Polgar, eds. Pp. 126–155.

Babb, Lawrence A. 1969. "Systemic Aspects of Chhatisgarhi Religion: An Analysis of a Regional Variant of Popular Hinduism." Unpublished doctoral dissertation, University of Rochester.

Balikçi, Asen. 1967. "Female Infanticide on the Arctic Coast." *Man* 2:615–625.

Bardhan, Pranab K. 1974. "On Life and Death Questions." *Economic and Political Weekly* Special Number 9(32–34):1293–1303.

Basu, Mahadeb. 1963. "On the Distribution of Sex Ratio in India." *Bulletin of the Cultural Research Institute* 2(2):53–55. Calcutta.

Basu, Tara Krishna. 1962. *The Bengal Peasant from Time to Time*. New York: Asia Publishing House.

Beals, Alan R. 1974. *Village Life in South India: Cultural Design and Environmental Variation*. Chicago: Aldine.

Beck, Brenda E. F. 1972. *Peasant Society in Koṅku: A Study of Right and Left Subcastes in South India*. Vancouver, Canada: University of British Columbia Press.

Beckerman, Stephen. 1976. "An Unusual Live-Birth Sex Ratio in Ecuador." *Social Biology* 23(2):172–174.

Béhar, Moisés. 1975. "The Role of Feeding and Nutrition in the Pathogeny and Prevention of Diarrheic Processes." *Bulletin of the Pan American Health Organization* 9(1):1–9.

Benedict, Burton. 1972. "Social Regulation of Fertility." In G. A. Harrison and A. J. Boyce, eds., *The Structure of Human Populations*. Oxford: Clarendon Press. Pp. 73–89.

Béteille, André. 1962. "Śripuram: A Village in Tanjore District." *Economic Weekly* 14:141–146.

————. 1966. *Caste, Class and Power: Changing Patterns of Stratification in a Tanjore Village*. Berkeley: University of California Press.

————. 1975. "The Position of Women in Indian Society." In Devaki Jain, ed., *Indian Women*. New Delhi: Director, Publications Division, Government of India. Pp. 59–68.

Bhalla, Promilla. 1964–1965. "Status, Role and Position of Women in Sakoh." Master's thesis, University of Delhi, India.

Birns, Beverly. 1978. "Women in Multiple Roles." Seminar presentation, Women's Studies Program. Syracuse University, Syracuse, N.Y.

Bochkov, N. P., and A. A. Kostrova. 1973. "Sex Ratio among Human Embryos and Newborns in a Russian Population." *Human Genetik* 17(2):91–98.

Boserup, Ester. 1970. *Women's Role in Economic Development*. New York: St. Martin's Press.

Bowles, Gordon T. 1953. "Population Control and the Family in Feudal and Post-Restoration Japan." *Kroeber Anthropological Society Papers 8–9*. Berkeley: The Kroeber Anthropological Society.

Brown, Judith K. 1970. "A Note on the Division of Labor by Sex." *American Anthropologist* 72(5):1074–1078.

Bruce, George. 1968. *The Stranglers: The Cult of Thuggee and Its Overthrow in British India*. New York: Harcourt, Brace and World.

Burkhart, Geoffrey L. 1969. "Agnatic Groups and Affinal Relations in a South Indian Caste: UDaiyaars of Salem District, Tamil Nadu." Unpublished doctoral dissertation, University of Rochester.

——. 1975. "Inheritance in South India: an 'Anomolous' Case." *Man in India* 55(2):85–97.

Burnes, Alexander. 1834. "On Female Infanticide in Cutch." *Journal of the Royal Asiatic Society* 1(2):193–199.

Calcutta Review. 1844. "Female Infanticide in Central and Western India." *Calcutta Review* 1(2):372–448.

Cantor/Atac. 1972. *"A Life Cycle": An Anthropological Study of Food Habits*. Report of the Tamil Nadu Nutrition Project. Madras, India.

Carstairs, G. Morris. 1975. "Village Women of Rajasthan." In Devaki Jain, ed., *Indian Women*. New Delhi: Director, Publications Division, Government of India. Pp. 231–235.

Cave-Browne, John. 1857. *Indian Infanticide: Its Origin, Progress and Suppression*. London: W. H. Allen.

Chauhan, Brij R. 1967. *A Rajasthan Village*. New Delhi: Vir Publishing House.

Chauhan, Virendra S. 1966. "'Agriculture-Population Complex' in the Jamuna Hindan Tract of Western Uttar Pradesh: A Micro-Regional Study in Spatial Inter-Relations of a Predominant Economic Activity, Demography and Cultural Landscape." Unpublished doctoral dissertation, University of Agra, India.

Claus, Peter J. 1970. "Kinship Organization of the Bant-Nadava Complex." Unpublished doctoral dissertation, Duke University.

Clements, Charles (Berkeley Health Project.) 1977. Personal communication, New Delhi.

Cohn, Bernard S. 1954. "The Camars of Senapur: A Study of the Changing Status of a Depressed Caste." Unpublished doctoral dissertation, Cornell University.

———. 1972. "The Changing Status of a Depressed Caste." In McKim Marriott, ed. *Village India: Studies in the Little Community*. Chicago: University of Chicago Press. Pp. 52–77.

Coleman, E. R. 1974. "L'infanticide dans le haut Moyen Age." *Annales, Economies, Sociétés, Civilisations* 29:315–335.

Crooke, William. 1971. *The Northwestern Provinces of India: Their History, Ethnology, and Administration*. Delhi: Indological Book House. (Reprint of 1897 edition.)

Dandekar, Kumudini. 1975. "Why has the Proportion of Women in India's Population Been Declining?" *Economic and Political Weekly* 10(42):1663–1667.

Dange, A. S. 1972. "An Analysis of Sex-Ratio Differentials by Regions of Madhya Pradesh." *Artha Vijnana* 14(3):273–286.

Das, M. N. 1956. "Female Infanticide among the Bedees and the Chouhans: Motives and Modes." *Man in India* 36(4):261–266.

———. 1957. "Movement to Suppress the Custom of Female Infanticide in the Punjab and Kashmir." *Man in India* 37(4)280–293.

Das Gupta, Monica. 1977. "From a Closed to an Open System: Fertility Behaviour in a Changing Indian Village." In T. Scarlett Epstein and Darrell Jackson, eds., *The Feasibility of Fertility Planning: Micro Perspectives*. New York: Pergamon Press. Pp. 97–121.

Davies, Christie. 1976. "The Relative Fertility of Hindus and Muslims." *Quest* 99:19–32.

Davis, Kingsley. 1946. "Human Fertility in India." *American Journal of Sociology* 52:243–254.

Davis, Kingsley, and Judith Blake. 1956. "Social Structure and Fertility: An Analytic Framework." *Economic Development and Cultural Change* 4:211–235.

Davis, Marvin G. 1975. "Rank and Rivalry in Rural West Bengal." Unpublished doctoral dissertation, University of Chicago.

Desai, P. B. 1967. "Variation in Population Sex Ratios in India, 1901–61." In Ashish Bose, ed., *Patterns of Population Change in India: 1951–1961*. New York: Allied Publishers. Pp. 372–388.

———. 1969. *Size and Sex Composition of the Population of India, 1901–1961*. New York: Asia Publishing House.

Dickeman, Mildred. 1975. "Demographic Consequences of Infanticide in Man." *Annual Review of Ecology and Systematics* 6:107–137.

——. 1976. "Infanticide and Hypergamy: A Neglected Relationship." Paper presented at the American Anthropological Association Meetings, San Francisco.

Divale, William. 1970. "Explanation for Primitive Warfare: Population Control and Significance of Primitive Sex Ratios." *New Scholar* 2(2):173–192.

——. 1971. "Ibo Population Control: The Ecology of Warfare and Social Organization." *California Anthropologist* 1:10–24.

Divale, William, and Marvin Harris. 1976. "Population, Warfare, and the Male Supremacist Complex." *American Anthropologist* 78:521–538.

Dixon, Ruth. 1978. *Rural Women at Work: Strategies for Development in South Asia*. Baltimore: Johns Hopkins University Press.

Djurfeldt, Göran, and Staffan Lindberg. 1975. *Behind Poverty: The Social Formation in a Tamil Village*. Scandinavian Institute of Asian Studies Monograph Series, No. 22. New Delhi: Oxford and IBH Publishing Co.

——. 1976. *Pills against Poverty: A Study of the Introduction of Western Medicine in a Tamil Village*. Scandinavian Institute of Asian Studies Monograph Series, No. 23. London: Curzon Press.

Douglas, Mary. 1966. "Population Control in Primitive Groups." *British Journal of Sociology* 17(3):263–273.

D'Souza, Victor S. 1975. "Family Status and Female Work Participation." In Alfred de Souza, ed., *Women in Contemporary India: Traditional Images and Changing Roles*. New Delhi: Indian Social Institute, Manohar. Pp. 129–141.

Dube, S. C. 1967. *Indian Village*. New York: Harper & Row.

Dumont, Louis. 1957a. *Hierarchy and Marriage Alliance in South Indian Kinship*. Occasional Papers of the Royal Anthropological Institute of Great Britain and Ireland, No. 12.

——. 1957b. *Une sous-caste de l'Inde du Sud: Organisation sociale et religion des Pramalai Kallar*. Paris: Mouton.

——. 1957c. "Kinship." *Contributions to Indian Sociology* 1:43–64.

——. 1959. "Dowry in Hindu Marriage." *Economic Weekly* 11:519–520.

——. 1961. "Marriage in India, the Present State of the Question. I. Marriage Alliance in South-East Asia and Ceylon." *Contributions to Indian Sociology* 5:74–95.

——. 1964. "Marriage in India. The Present State of the Question: Postscript to Part I.—II. Nayar and Newar." *Contributions to Indian Sociology* 7:77–98.

——. 1966. "Marriage in India—The Present State of the Question. III.

North India in Relation to South India." *Contributions to Indian Sociology* 9:90–114.

Dutta, Jatindra M. 1961. "Was There a Shortage of Women in Ancient India?" *Man in India* 41(3):184–193.

El-Badry, M. A. 1969. "Higher Female than Male Mortality in Some Countries of South Asia: A Digest." *Journal of the American Statistical Association* 64:1234–1244.

Fitzgerald, Thomas K., ed. 1977. *Nutrition and Anthropology in Action.* Assen/Amsterdam: Van Gorcum.

Ford, Clellan S. 1964. *A Comparative Study of Human Reproduction.* Yale University Publications in Anthropology No. 32. New Haven, Conn.: HRAF Press.

Fraiburg, Selma. 1977. *Every Child's Birthright: In Defense of Mothering.* New York: Basic Books.

Freed, Ruth S. 1971. "The Legal Process in a Village in North India: The Case of Maya." *Transactions of the New York Academy of Sciences* 33:423–435.

Freed, Stanley A., and Ruth S. Freed. 1971. "The Relationship between Fertility and Selected Social Factors in a North Indian Village." *Man in India* 51:274–290.

——. 1973. "Status and the Spatial Range of Marriages in a North Indian Area." *Anthropological Quarterly* 46(2):92–99.

——. 1976. *Shanti Nagar: The Effects of Urbanization in a Village in North India: 1. Social Organization.* Anthropological Papers of the American Museum of Natural History, Volume 53, Part 1. New York: The American Museum of Natural History.

Freeman, Milton R. 1971. "Social and Ecologic Analysis of Systematic Female Infanticide among the Netsilik Eskimo." *American Anthropologist* 73(5):1011–1018.

Friedl, Ernestine. 1959. "Dowry and Inheritance in Modern Greece." *Transactions of the New York Academy of Sciences* Series II, 22(1):49–54.

——. 1975. *Women and Men: An Anthropologist's View.* New York: Holt, Rinehart and Winston.

Fukutake, Tadashi, Tsutomu Ouchi, and Chie Nakane. 1964. *The Socio-Economic Structure of the Indian Village.* Tokyo: Institute of Asian Economic Affairs.

Fuller, Christopher J. 1976. *The Nayars Today.* New York: Cambridge University Press.

——. 1978. Questionnaire response.

Gadgil, D. R. 1965. *Women in the Working Force in India.* New York: Asia Publishing House.

Gardner, Lytt I. 1972. "Deprivation Dwarfism." *Scientific American* 227(1):76–82.

Gebre-Medhin, Mehari, Stephen Gurovsky, and Lars Bondestam. 1976. "Association of Maternal Age and Parity with Birth Weight, Sex Ratio, Stillbirths and Multiple Births." (*Journal of Tropical Pediatrics and*) *Environmental Child Health* 22(3):99–102.

Ghadimi, Hossein. 1957. "Child Care in Iran." *Journal of Pediatrics* 50:620–628.

Ghosh, B. M. 1966. "Feeding Habits of Infants and Children in South India." *Indian Journal of Medical Research* Sept.:880–897.

Gokulanathan, K. S., and K. P. Verghese. 1969. "Socio-Cultural Malnutrition (Growth Failure in Children due to Socio-Cultural Factors)." (*Journal of Tropical Pediatrics and*) *Environmental Child Health* 15(3):118–124.

Goldschmidt, Walter. 1959. *Man's Way: A Preface to the Understanding of Human Society.* New York: World.

Goldschmidt, Walter, and Evalyn Jacobson Kunkel. 1971. "The Structure of the Peasant Family." *American Anthropologist* 73(5):1058–1076.

Goody, Jack. 1973. "Bridewealth and Dowry in Africa and Eurasia." In J. Goody and S. J. Tambiah, eds., *Bridewealth and Dowry.* New York: Cambridge University Press. Pp. 1–58.

——. 1976. *Production and Reproduction: A Comparative Study of the Domestic Domain.* Cambridge Studies in Social Anthropology, No. 17. New York: Cambridge University Press.

Goon, A. M. 1975. "Sex-Ratio and Indian Birth Registration Data." *Indian Journal of Public Health* 19(1):34–37.

Gopalan, C., and A. Nadamuni Naidu. 1972. "Nutrition and Fertility." *The Lancet* 2:1077–1079.

Gordon, John E., Sohan Singh, and John B. Wyon. 1965. "Causes of Death at Different Ages by Sex and by Season in a Rural Population of Punjab 1957–59." *Indian Journal of Medical Research* Sept.:906–917.

Gosal, Gurdev S. 1961. "The Regionalism of Sex Composition of India's Population." *Rural Sociology* 26(2):122–137.

Gough, E. Kathleen. 1956. "Brahman Kinship in a Tamil Village." *American Anthropologist* 58:826–853.

Gould, Harold A. 1959. "Family and Kinship in a North Indian Village." Unpublished doctoral dissertation, Washington University.

——. 1960. "The Micro-Demography of Marriages in a North Indian Area." *Southwestern Journal of Anthropology* 16:476–491.

Gould, Ketayun H. 1976. "The Twain Never Met: Sherupur, India, and the Family Planning Program." In Marshall and Polgar, eds. Pp. 184–203.

Granzberg, Gary. 1973. "Twin Infanticide: A Cross-Cultural Test of a Materialist Explanation." *Ethos* 4:405–412.

Greenough, Paul R. 1977. "Mortality due to the Bengal Famine of 1943–44: The Available Data and Their Interpretation." Paper presented at the Midwestern Meeting of the Association for Asian Studies, De Kalb, Illinois.

———. 1978. Personal communication.

———. 1982 (forthcoming). *Prosperity and Misery in Modern India: The Bengal Famine of 1943–1944*. New York: Oxford University Press.

Grewal, Tina, Tara Gopaldas, and V. J. Gadre. 1973. "Etiology of Malnutrition in Rural Indian Preschool Children (Madhya Pradesh)." (*Journal of Tropical Pediatrics and*) *Environmental Child Health* 19(3):265–270.

Gulati, Leela. 1975. "Female Work Participation: A Study of Inter-State Differences." *Economic and Political Weekly* 10(1 and 2):35–42.

Gulhati, Ravi. 1978. "India's Population Policy: Critical Issues for the Future." *Public Policy* 26(3):415–454.

Gupta, Giri Raj. 1974. *Marriage, Religion and Society: Pattern of Change in an Indian Village*. New York: John Wiley.

Haldar, A. K., and N. Bhattacharyya. 1969. "Fertility and Sex-Sequence of Children of Indian Couples." *Sankhyā* Series B, 31:144.

Hanks, Lucien M. 1972. *Rice and Man: Agricultural Ecology in Southeast Asia*. New York: Aldine-Atherton.

Harper, Edward B. 1958. "Economic Structure of a South Indian Village." Unpublished doctoral dissertation, Cornell University.

———. 1968. "Social Consequences of an 'Unsuccessful' Low Caste Movement." In James Silverberg, ed., *Social Mobility and the Caste System in India: An Interdisciplinary Symposium*. Comparative Studies in Society and History Supplement III. The Hague: Mouton. Pp. 36–65.

Harries, J. T. 1976. "The Problem of Bacterial Diarrhoea." *CIBA Foundation Symposium* New Series 42:3–25.

Harris, Marvin. 1974. *Cows, Pigs, Wars and Witches: The Riddles of Culture*. New York: Vintage Press.

———. 1975. *Culture, People and Nature*. New York: Thomas Y. Crowell.

Hasan, Khwaja A. 1971. "Hindu Dietary Practices and Culinary Rituals in a North Indian Village." *Ethnomedicine* 1(1):43–70.

Hecht, Julia A. 1972. "The Case of the Missing Bride: Female Infanticide in Mid-Nineteenth Century, North India." Unpublished master's thesis, University of Chicago.

Hiebert, Paul G. 1971. *Konduru: Structure and Integration in a South Indian Village*. Minneapolis: University of Minnesota Press.

Hirschfeld, Lawrence A., James Howe, and Bruce Levin. 1978. "Warfare, Infanticide, and Statistical Inference: A Comment on Divale and Harris." *American Anthropologist* 80:110–115.

Hitchcock, John T. 1956. "The Rajputs of Khaalaapur: A Study of Kinship, Social Stratification and Politics." Unpublished doctoral dissertation, Cornell University.

Indian Council of Medical Research. 1972. *Growth and Physical Development of Indian Infants and Children*. New Delhi: Indian Council of Medical Research.

Jacobson, Doranne. 1970. "Hidden Faces: Hindu and Muslim Purdah in a Central Indian Village." Unpublished doctoral dissertation, Columbia University.

———. 1972. "You Have Given Us a Goddess: Flexibility in Central Indian Kinship." Paper presented at the American Anthropological Association Meetings, Toronto.

Jadhav, Malati, and S. J. Baker. 1961. "A Study of the Etiology of Severe Anaemia in 50 Children." *Indian Journal of Child Health* 10:235–243.

Jelliffe, Derrick B. 1957. "Social Culture and Nutrition: Cultural Blocks and Protein Malnutrition in Early Childhood in West Bengal." *Pediatrics* 20:128–138.

———. 1966. *The Assessment of the Nutritional Status of the Community*. Geneva, Switzerland: World Health Organization.

———. 1968. *Infant Nutrition in the Subtropics and Tropics*. Geneva, Switzerland: World Health Organization.

Jyothi, K. K., R. Dhakshayani, M. C. Swaminathan, and P. S. Venkatachalam. 1963. "A Study of the Socio-Economic, Diet and Nutritional Status of a Rural Community near Hyderabad." *Tropical and Geographical Medicine* 15:403–410.

Kang, Yung Sun, and Wan Kyoo Cho. 1962. "The Sex Ratio at Birth and Other Attributes of the Newborn from Maternity Hospitals in Korea." *Human Biology* 34(1):38–40.

Kar, Barbara. 1968. *Nutrition Research Profile: India*. New Delhi: U.S. Agency for International Development.

Karve, Irawati. 1968. *Kinship Organization in India*. New York: Asia Publishing House.

Kellum, Barbara A. 1973. "Infanticide in England in the Later Middle Ages." *History of Childhood Quarterly: Journal of Psychohistory* 1(3):367–388.

Kelly, Narinder O. 1975. "Some Socio-Cultural Correlates of Indian Sex Ratios: Case Studies of Punjab and Kerala." Unpublished doctoral dissertation, University of Pennsylvania.

Khan, M. E. 1973. "Factors Affecting Spacing of Births." *Journal of Family Welfare* 20:54–67.

King, Christopher R. 1977. "The Silent Words: Food Transactions in Hindi Literature." Unpublished paper, University of Windsor, Canada.

Klausen, Arne M. 1968. *Kerala Fishermen and the Indo-Norwegian Pilot Project.* Oslo: Scandinavian University Books, Universitetsforlaget.

Kolenda, Pauline M. 1968. "Region, Caste, and Family Structure: A Comparative Study of the Indian 'Joint' Family." In Milton Singer and Bernard S. Cohn, eds., *Structure and Change in Indian Society.* Viking Fund Publications in Anthropology No. 47. New York: Wenner-Gren Foundation for Anthropological Research. Pp. 339–396.

———. 1971. "Regional Differences in Indian Family Structure." In Robert Crane, ed., *Regions and Regionalism in South Asian Studies.* Durham, N.C.: Duke University Press. Pp. 147–226.

Kumbhat, M. M. 1959. "Anaemias in Infancy and Childhood." *Indian Journal of Child Health* 8:113–115.

Lang, Olga. 1946. *Chinese Family and Society.* New Haven: Yale University Press.

Langer, William L. 1973. "Infanticide: A Historical Survey." *History of Childhood Quarterly: Journal of Psychohistory* 1(3):353–365.

Leaf, Murray J. 1972. *Information and Behavior in a Sikh Village: Social Organization Reconsidered.* Berkeley: University of California Press.

———. 1978. Questionnaire response.

Lee, Sung, and Kiichi Takano. 1970. "Sex Ratios in Human Embryos Obtained from Induced Abortion: Histological Examination of the Gonad in 1,452 Cases." *American Journal of Obstetrics and Gynecology* 108(8):1294–1296.

LeVine, Robert A. 1977. "Child Rearing as Cultural Adaption." In Herbert P. Leiderman, Steven R. Tulkin, and Anne Rosenfeld, eds., *Culture and Infancy: Variations in the Human Experience.* New York: Academic Press. Pp. 15–27.

Levinson, Franklin J. 1972. "An Economic Analysis of Malnutrition among Young Children in Rural India." Unpublished doctoral dissertation, Cornell University.

Lewis, Oscar. 1965. *Village Life in Northern India: Studies in a Delhi Village.* New York: Random House. Vintage Books.

Libbee, Michael J., and David E. Sopher. 1975. "Marriage Migration in Rural India." In Leszek A. Kosinski and R. Mansell Prothero, eds., *People on the Move: Studies on Internal Migration.* London: Methuen. Pp. 347–359.

———. 1980. "Territorial Endogamy and the Spatial Structure of Marriage in

India." In David E. Sopher, ed., *An Exploration of India: Geographical Perspectives on Society and Culture*. Ithaca, N.Y.: Cornell University Press. Pp. 65–104.

Lindenbaum, Shirley. 1977. "The 'Last Course': Nutrition and Anthropology in Asia." In Thomas K. Fitzgerald, ed., *Nutrition and Anthropology in Action*. Assen/Amsterdam: Van Gorcum. Pp. 141–155.

Lozoff, Betsy, K. R. Kamath, and R. A. Feldman. 1975. "Infection and Disease in South Indian Families: Beliefs about Childhood Diarrhea." *Human Organization* 34(4):353–358.

Luschinsky, Mildred S. 1962. "The Life of Women in a Village of North India: A Study of Role and Status." Unpublished doctoral dissertation, Cornell University.

Madan, T. N. 1965. *Family and Kinship: A Study of the Pandits of Rural Kashmir*. New York: Asia Publishing House.

Mahar, Michael. 1966. "Marriage Networks in the Gangetic Plain." Unpublished doctoral dissertation, Cornell University.

Maharaja Sayajirao University of Baroda. 1970. *Social Change and Perception of Change in Child Rearing Practices in a Suburban Indian Village*. Baroda: Maharaja Sayajirao University of Baroda Press.

Majumdar, D. N. 1947. *The Matrix of Indian Culture*. Lucknow, India: Universal Publishers.

———. 1954. "About Women in Patrilocal Societies in South Asia." In A. Appadorai, ed., *Status of Women in South Asia*. London: Longmans.

———. 1958. *Caste and Communication in an Indian Village*. New York: Asia Publishing House.

Mamdani, Mahmood. 1972. *The Myth of Population Control: Family, Caste, and Class in an Indian Village*. New York: Monthly Review Press.

Manchandra, S. S., and H. L. Khanna. 1962. "Severe Anaemias in Children (an Analysis of 105 cases)." *Indian Journal of Child Health* 11(10):463–484.

Manchandra, S. S., and K. K. Sachdeva. 1962. "Morbidity and Mortality in Children in North India (Punjab)." *Indian Journal of Pediatrics* 29:333–350.

Mandelbaum, David G. 1974. *Human Fertility in India: Social Components and Policy Perspectives*. Berkeley: University of California Press.

Marshall, John F. 1972. "Culture and Contraception: Response Determinants to a Family Planning Program in a North Indian Village." Unpublished doctoral dissertation, University of Hawaii.

———. 1978. Questionnaire response.

Marshall, John F., Susan Morris, and Steven Polgar. 1972. "Culture and

Natality: A Preliminary Classified Bibliography." *Current Anthropology* 13(2):268–278.

Marshall, John F., and Steven Polgar, eds. 1976. *Culture, Natality and Family Planning.* Carolina Population Center Monograph No. 21. Chapel Hill: University of North Carolina.

Mata, L. J., et al. 1976. "Breast-Feeding, Weaning and the Diarrheal Syndrome in a Guatemalan Indian Village." *CIBA Foundation Symposium* New Series 42:311–338.

Mathen, K. K. 1962. "Preliminary Lessons Learned from the Rural Population Control Study of Singur." In Clyde V. Kiser, ed., *Research in Family Planning.* Princeton: Princeton University Press. Pp. 33–50.

Mathew, N. T. 1947. "Factors Influencing the Relative Proportion at Birth of the Two Sexes." *Sankhyā* Series A 8(3):277–281.

Matthiessen, P. C., and M. E. Matthiessen. 1977. "Sex Ratio in a Sample of Human Fetuses in Denmark, 1962–1973." *Annals of Human Biology* 4(2):183–185.

May, D. A., and D. M. Heer. 1968. "Son Survivorship Motivation and Family Size in India." *Population Studies* 22(2):199–210.

May, Jacques M. 1961. *The Ecology of Malnutrition in the Far and Near East (Food Resources, Habits, and Deficiencies).* New York: Hafner.

Mayer, Adrian C. 1970. *Caste and Kinship in Central India: A Village and Its Region.* Berkeley: University of California Press.

McClelland, Gary H. 1979. "Determining the Impact of Sex Preferences on Fertility: A Consideration of Parity Progression Ratio, Dominance, and Stopping Rule Measures." *Demography* 16(3):377–388.

Meek, Ronald L., ed. 1971. *Marx and Engels on the Population Bomb.* Berkeley: Ramparts Press.

Mencher, Joan P. 1963. "Growing Up in South Malabar." *Human Organization* 22:54–65.

———. 1966. "Namboodiri Brahmans: An Analysis of a Traditional Elite in Kerala." *Journal of Asian and African Studies* 1(3):183–196.

———. 1970. "A Tamil Village: Changing Socioeconomic Structure in Madras State." In K. Ishwaran, ed., *Change and Continuity in India's Villages.* New York: Columbia University Press. Pp. 192–218.

———. 1977. "Women and Rice Cultivation in South India." Unpublished paper, Herbert Lehman College, New York.

Mikamo, Kazuya. 1969. "Female Preponderance in the Sex Ratio during Early Intra-Uterine Development: A Sex Chromatin Study." *Japanese Journal of Human Genetics* 13(4):272–277.

Miller, D. B. 1975. *From Hierarchy to Stratification: Changing Patterns of*

Social Inequality in a North Indian Village. Delhi: Oxford University Press.

Minturn, Leigh. 1976. "Village Women: 1954–1974." Paper presented at the Association of Asian Studies Meeting, Toronto, Canada.

Minturn, Leigh, and John T. Hitchcock. 1966. *The Rājpūts of Khalapur, India*. Six Cultures Series, Vol. III. New York: John Wiley.

Moffatt, Michael. 1978. Questionnaire response.

——. 1979. *An Untouchable Community in South India: Structure and Consensus*. Princeton, N.J.: Princeton University Press.

Montgomery, Edward. 1972. "Stratification and Nutrition in a Population of Southern India." Unpublished doctoral dissertation, Columbia University.

Moore, Mick. 1973. "Cross-Cultural Surveys of Peasant Family Structures: Some Comments." *American Anthropologist* 75(3):911–915.

Morrison, Charles. 1965. "Dispute in Dhara: A Study of Village Politics in Eastern Punjab." Unpublished doctoral dissertation, University of Chicago.

Mukerji, A. B., and S. Mehta. 1975. "Female Participation in Agricultural Labor in India: Patterns and Associations." *Tijdschrift voor Economische en Sociale Geografie* 66(2):103–107.

Murray, Gerald F. 1976. "Women in Perdition: Ritual Fertility Control in Haiti." In Marshall and Polgar, eds. Pp. 59–78.

Nag, A. C. 1951. "Study of Variation in Sex-Ratio." *Calcutta Statistical Association Bulletin* 3(12):139–144.

Nag, Moni. 1967. "Family Type and Fertility." *Proceedings of the World Population Conference 1965*, 2:160–163. New York: United Nations.

——. 1968. *Factors Affecting Human Fertility in Nonindustrial Societies: A Cross-Cultural Study*. Yale University Publications in Anthropology, No. 66. New Haven: HRAF Press.

——. 1973. "Population Anthropology: Problems and Perspectives." In Morton Fried, ed., *Explorations in Anthropology*. New York: Thomas Y. Crowell. Pp. 254–274.

Natarajan, D. 1971. *Changes in Sex Ratio*. Census Centenary Monograph No. 6. New Delhi: Office of the Registar General.

Nath, Kamla. 1968. "Women in the Working Force in India." *Economic and Political Weekly* Aug. (3):1205–1213.

Nath, Viswa. 1973. "Female Infanticide and the Lewa Kanbis of Gujarat in the Nineteenth Century." *Indian Economic and Social History Review* 10(4):386–404.

Neave, E. R. 1910. *Mainpuri: A District Gazetteer*. Vol. 10 of District

Gazetteers of the United Provinces of Agra and Oudh. Allahabad: Superintendent, Government Press, Uttar Pradesh.

Newell, K. R., et al. 1976. "Diarrheal Diseases of Infancy in Cali, Colombia: Study Design and Summary Report on Isolated Disease Agents." *Bulletin of the Pan American Health Organization* 10(2):143–155.

Newell, William H. 1952. "Gaddi Kinship and Affinal Terms." *Man in India* 32(2):86–110.

——. 1965. *Himachal Pradesh: Report of Scheduled Castes and Scheduled Tribes (A Study of the Gaddi—Scheduled Tribe—and Affiliated Castes).* Census of India 1961. Part V-B. Vol. XX.

——. 1978. Questionnaire response.

Newland, Kathleen. 1979. *The Sisterhood of Man: The Impact of Women's Changing Roles on Social and Economic Life around the World.* New York: Norton.

Oakley, Ann. 1972. *Sex, Gender, and Society.* New York: Harper & Row.

O'Dwyer, Michael (Sir). 1925. *India as I Knew It.* London: Constable.

Oldham, C. E. A., ed. 1930. *Journal of Francis Buchanan: Kept during the Survey of the Districts of Bhagalpur in 1810–11.* Patna, India: Superintendent, Government Printing.

O'Malley, L. S. S. 1975. *India's Social Heritage.* New York: Octagon Books. (Reprint of 1934 edition.)

Orenstein, Henry. 1965. *Gaon: Conflict and Cohesion in an Indian Village.* Princeton: Princeton University Press.

Pakrasi, Kanti B. 1964. "Note on Differential Sex-Ratios and Polyandrous People in India." *Man in India* 44(2):161–174.

——. 1968. "On Female Infanticide in India." *Bulletin of the Cultural Research Institute* 7:33–48.

——. 1970. "Infanticide, Vital Statistics and Proclaimed Castes of India." *Bulletin, Socio-Economic Research Institute* (Calcutta) 4(1 and 2):81–98.

Pakrasi, Kanti B., and Ajit Halder. 1971. "Sex Ratios and Sex Sequences of Births in India." *Journal of Biosocial Science* 3:377–387.

Pakrasi, Kanti B., and B. Sasmal. 1971. "Infanticide and Variation of Sex-Ratio in a Caste Population of India." *Acta Medica Auxologica* (Italy) 3(3):217–228.

Pande, R. C. 1976. "Bacteriology of Infantile Diarrhoea and Gastroenteritis in Allahabad." *Indian Journal of Pathological Microbiology* 19(3):169–177.

Pandey, Raj B. 1961. *Hindu Samskaras.* Delhi: Motilal Banarsidass.

Panigrahi, Lalita. 1976. *British Social Policy and Female Infanticide in India.* New Delhi: Munshiram Manoharlal.

Papanek, Hanna. 1971. "Purdah in Pakistan: Seclusion and Modern Occupations for Women." *Journal of Marriage and the Family* 33(3):517–530.

Parks, Fanny. 1975. *Wanderings of a Pilgrim in Search of the Picturesque*. Karachi: Oxford University Press. (Reprint of 1850 edition.)

Pathare, Rajani. 1966. "The Family Planning Programme: A Sociological Analysis." *Sociological Bulletin* 15(2):44–62.

Piers, Maria. 1978. *Infanticide*. New York: Norton.

Pike, Kenneth L. 1969. *Language in Relation to a Unified Theory of the Structure of Human Behavior*. Janua Linguarum Series Maior XXIV. The Hague: Mouton.

Planalp, Jack M. 1956. "Religious Life and Values in an Indian Village." Unpublished doctoral dissertation, Cornell University.

——. 1971. *Heat Stress and Culture in North India*. Natick, Mass.: U.S. Army Research Institute of Environmental Medicine, Special Technical Report.

Pocock, David F. 1972. *Kanbi and Patidar: A Study of the Patidar Community of Gujarat*. New York: Oxford University Press.

Poffenberger, Thomas. 1968. "Motivational Aspects of Resistance to Family Planning in an Indian Village." *Demography* 5:757–766.

——. 1975. *Fertility and Family Life in an Indian Village*. Michigan Papers on South and Southeast Asia No. 10. Ann Arbor: Center for South and Southeast Asian Studies, University of Michigan.

Pradhan, M. C. 1966. *The Political System of the Jats of North India*. New York: Oxford University Press.

Preston, Samuel H. 1976. *Mortality Patterns in National Populations: With Special Reference to Recorded Causes of Death*. New York: Academic Press.

Prothro, Edwin T. 1967. *Child Rearing in the Lebanon*. Harvard Middle Eastern Monographs VIII. Cambridge, Mass.: Harvard University Press.

Pryor, Frederic L. 1977. *The Origins of the Economy: A Comparative Study of Distribution in Primitive and Peasant Economies*. New York: Academic Press.

Radbill, Samuel X. 1968. "A History of Child Abuse and Infanticide." In R. E. Helfer and C. H. Kempe, eds., *The Battered Child*. Chicago: University of Chicago Press. Pp. 3–21.

Raikes, Charles. 1852. *Notes on the North-Western Provinces of India*. London: Chapman and Hall.

Ramachandran, K. V., and Vinayak A. Deshpande. 1964. "The Sex Ratio at Birth in India by Regions." *Milbank Memorial Quarterly* 42(2):84–95.

Ramachandran, R. S., and S. Purnayyam. 1966. "Tuberculosis in Indian Children." *Indian Pediatrics* 3(6):218–223.

Rao, B. R. H., et al. 1961. "Nutrition Status Survey of the Rural Population of Sholavarum: Seasonal Diet Survey." *Indian Journal of Medical Research* 49:316–326.

Rao, D. Hanumantha, and S. C. Balasubramanian. 1966. "Socio-Cultural Aspects of Infant Feeding Practices in a Telengana Village." *Tropical and Geographical Medicine* 18:353–360.

Raphael, Dana. 1973. *The Tender Gift: Breastfeeding.* Englewood Cliffs, N.J.: Prentice-Hall.

Reddy, D. Narasimha. 1975. "Female Work Participation: A Study of Inter-State Differences, A Comment." *Economic and Political Weekly* 10(23):902–905.

Reeves, P. D., ed. 1971. *Sleeman in Oudh: An Abridgement of W. H. Sleeman's A Journey through the Kingdom of Oude in 1849–50.* London: Cambridge University Press.

Regelson, Stanley. 1972. "Some Aspects of Food Behavior in a South Indian Village." Unpublished doctoral dissertation, Columbia University.

Reid, Russell M. 1971. "Marriage Patterns, Demography and Population Genetics in a South Indian Caste: A Study of Inbreeding in a Human Population." Unpublished doctoral dissertation, University of Illinois at Urbana-Champaign.

———. 1978. Questionnaire response.

Reith, David J. 1975. "Structural and Regional Bases of Sex Ratios in the Population of India." Unpublished doctoral dissertation, University of Illinois at Urbana-Champaign.

Risley, Herbert (Sir). 1969. *The People of India.* Delhi: Oriental Books Reprint Corporation. (Reprint of 1915 edition.)

Rohde, Jon E., and Robert S. Northrup. 1976. "Taking Science Where the Diarrhoea Is." *CIBA Foundation Symposium* New Series 42:339–358.

Rohner, Ronald P. 1975. *They Love Me, They Love Me Not: A Worldwide Study of the Effects of Parental Acceptance and Rejection.* New Haven, Conn.: HRAF Press.

Roy, Manisha. 1975. *Bengali Women.* Chicago: Chicago University Press.

Rukanuddin, Abdul R. 1967. "A Study of the Sex Ratio in Pakistan." In Warren C. Robinson, ed., *Studies in the Demography of Pakistan.* Karachi: Pakistan Institute of Development Economics. Pp. 140–225.

Schwartzberg, Joseph E. 1961. *Occupational Structure and Levels of Economic Development in India: A Regional Analysis.* 1961 Census of India. Monograph No. 4. Delhi: Office of the Registrar General.

———. 1978. *A History Atlas of India.* Association for Asian Studies Reference Series, 2. Chicago: University of Chicago Press.

Scrimshaw, Nevin S., Carl E. Taylor, and John E. Gordon. 1968. *Interactions of Nutrition and Infection.* Geneva, Switzerland: World Health Organization.

Sharma, S. K., R. K. Taluja, P. S. Manjerekar, and K. K. Kaul. 1968. "Diarrhoea in Jabalpur: Bacteriologic Study and Therapeutic Trials." *Indian Pediatrics* 5(4):154–160.

Shukla, N. K. 1976. *The Social Structure of an Indian Village*. New Delhi: Cosmo Publications.

Siddiqui, Nafis A. 1976. *Population Geography of Muslims of India*. New Delhi: S. Chand and Company Pvt. Ltd.

Sidhu, L. S., and S. Anand. 1972. "Secondary Sex Ratio in a Punjabi Population." *Eastern Anthropologist* 25(1):29–37.

Singh, Indera P. 1971. "A Sikh Village." *Journal of American Folklore* 71:479–503.

Singh, Tulja R. 1969. *The Madiga: A Study in Social Structure and Change*. Lucknow, India: Ethnographic and Folk Culture Society, Uttar Pradesh.

Sivertsen, Dagfinn. 1963. *When Caste Barriers Fall: A Study of Social and Economic Change in a South Indian Village*. New York: Humanities Press and Oslo: Universitetsforlaget.

Smith, Thomas C. 1977. *Nakahara: Family Farming and Population in a Japanese Village, 1717–1830*. Stanford, Calif.: Stanford University Press.

Sopher, David E. 1974. "A Measure of Disparity." *The Professional Geographer* 26(4):389–392.

——. 1979. "Temporal Disparity as a Measure of Change." *The Professional Geographer* 31(4):377–381.

——. 1980. "The Geographical Patterning of Culture in India." In David E. Sopher, ed., *An Exploration of India: Geographical Perspectives on Society and Culture*. Ithaca, N.Y.: Cornell University Press. Pp. 289–326.

Spring, Anita. 1976. "An Indigenous Therapeutic Style and Its Consequences for Natality: the Luvale of Zambia." In Marshall and Polgar, eds. Pp. 99–125.

Srinivas, M. N. 1976. *The Remembered Village*. Berkeley: University of California Press.

Srivastava, A. K., J. K. Bhatnagar, B. G. Prasad, and N. L. Sharma. 1973. "A Clinical and Aetiological Study of Diarrhoea in Hospitalized Children in Lucknow." *Indian Journal of Medical Research* 61(4):596–602.

Stein, Dorothy K. 1978. "Women to Burn: Suttee as a Normative Institution." *Signs* 4(2):253–268.

Stern, C. 1960. *Principles of Human Genetics*. San Francisco: W. H. Freeman.

Stevenson, A. C., and M. Bobrow. 1967. "Determinants of Sex Proportions in Man, with Consideration of the Evidence Concerning a Contribution from X-Linked Mutations to Intrauterine Death." *Journal of Medical Genetics* 4:190–196.

Sundar Rao, P. S. S. 1978. Unpublished findings of the Vellore Project, Vellore, Madras.

Swaminathan, M. C. 1976. "Nutrition in India." In Donald S. McLaren, ed., *Nutrition in the Community*. New York: Wiley. Pp. 321–344.

Tambiah, S. J. 1973. "Dowry and Bridewealth and the Property Rights of Women in South Asia." In Jack Goody and S. J. Tambiah, eds., *Bridewealth and Dowry*. New York: Cambridge University Press. Pp. 59–169.

Taylor, Richard W. 1969. "Hindu Religious Values and Family Planning." *Religion and Society* 16:6–22.

Thurston, Edgar. 1975. *Ethnographic Notes in Southern India*. Delhi: Cosmo Publications. (Reprint of 1907 edition.)

Timmer, Maarten. 1961. *Child Mortality and Population Pressure in the D. I. Jogjakarta, Java, Indonesia: A Socio-Medical Study*. Rotterdam: Bronder-Offset.

Tod, James. 1971. *Annals and Antiquities of Rajasthan: Or the Central Western Rajput States of India*. Delhi: Motilal Banarsidass. (Reprint of 1920 edition.)

Trexler, R. C. 1973. "Infanticide in Florence: New Sources and First Results." *History of Childhood Quarterly: Journal of Psychohistory* 1(1):98–116.

United Nations. 1961. *The Mysore Population Study*. Population Studies No. 34. Department of Economic and Social Affairs. New York: United Nations.

——. 1976. *Demographic Yearbook 1975*. New York: United Nations.

——. 1977. "New United Nations Predictions: A Brief Summary of the Projections of the Total Population as Assessed in 1973–1974." *Population Bulletin of the United Nations* 8:97–106.

Veen, K. W. van der. 1972. *I Give Thee My Daughter: A Study of Marriage and Hierarchy among the Anavil Brahmans of South Gujarat*. Assen: Royal Van Gorcum.

Visaria, Pravin M. 1961. *The Sex Ratio of the Population of India*. 1961 Census of India. Vol. I. Mongraph 10. New Delhi: Office of the Registrar General.

——. 1967a. "The Sex Ratio of the Population of India and Pakistan and Regional Variation during 1901–1961." In Ashish Bose, ed., *Pattern of Population Change in India 1951–1961*. New York: Allied Publishers. Pp. 334–371.

——. 1967b. "Sex Ratio at Birth in Territories with a Relatively Complete Registration." *Eugenics Quarterly* 14(2):132–142.

Wadley, Susan S. 1975. *Shakti: Power in the Conceptual Structure of*

Karimpur Religion. University of Chicago Studies in Anthropology. Series in Social, Cultural, and Linguistic Anthropology, No. 2. Chicago: Department of Anthropology, University of Chicago.

——. 1977. Personal communication.

Wadley, Susan S., and Bruce W. Derr. 1978. Questionnaire response.

Weir, J. A. 1973. "Sex Ratio." Part IV of "Sex." *Encyclopaedia Britannica.* Volume 20. Pp. 293–295.

Whyte, Robert O. 1974. *Rural Nutrition in Monsoon Asia.* New York: Oxford University Press.

Williamson, Laila. 1978. "Infanticide: An Anthropological Analysis." In Marvin Kohl, ed., *Infanticide and the Value of Life.* Buffalo, N.Y.: Prometheus Books. Pp. 61–75.

Williamson, Nancy. 1976. *Sons or Daughters: A Cross-Cultural Survey of Parental Preferences.* Beverly Hills: Sage Publications.

——. 1978. "Boys or Girls? Parents' Preferences and Sex Control." *Population Bulletin* 33(1):1–35.

Wiltse Harper, Judith. 1971. "Divarus of the Malnad." Unpublished doctoral dissertation, University of Washington.

Winzeler, Robert L. 1974. "Sex Role Equality, Wet Rice Cultivation and the State in Southeast Asia." *American Anthropologist* 76:563–565.

Wiser, Charlotte V. 1936. *The Foods of a Hindu Village of North India.* Allahabad, India: Superintendent, Printing and Stationery.

——. 1978. *Four Families of Karimpur.* Foreign and Comparative Studies/South Asian Series No. 3. Syracuse: Maxwell School of Citizenship and Public Affairs, Syracuse University.

Wiser, William, and Charlotte Wiser. 1971. *Behind Mud Walls 1930–1960: With a Sequel, The Village in 1970.* Berkeley: University of California Press.

Wyon, John B., and John E. Gordon. 1971. *The Khanna Study: Population Problems in the Punjab.* Cambridge, Mass.: Harvard University Press.

Yamamoto, M., T. Ito, and G. J. Watanabe. 1977. "Determination of Prenatal Sex Ratio in Man." *Human Genetics* 36(3):265–269.

Youseff, Nadia H. 1971. "Social Structure and the Female Labor Force: The Case of Women Workers in Muslim Middle Eastern Countries." *Demography* 8(4):427–439.

——. 1974. *Women and Work in Developing Societies.* Monograph Series No. 15. University of California Institute of International Studies.

Census of India Sources

India. 1873. *Census Northwest Provinces 1871*. Allahabad.

———. 1875. *Census 1872 General Report*. London.

———. 1881. *Census 1881 Report on the Census of British India*. London.

———. 1903. *Census 1901 India*. Calcutta.

———. 1933. *Census 1931 India*. Delhi.

———. 1933. *Census 1931 Madras*. Delhi.

———. 1933. *Census 1931 United Provinces*. Delhi.

———. 1961. *Census of India 1961*. Delhi: Office of the Manager of Publications.

    Vol. VIII. *Kerala*. Part VI A: Village Survey Monographs. A, *Cannanore and Kozhikode Districts*; B, *Palghat and Trichur Districts*; C, *Ernakulam and Kottayam Districts*; D, *Alleppey District*; E, *Quilon District*; F, *Trivandrum District*.

    Vol. IX. *Madras*. Part IV: Village Survey Monographs. 9, *Thadagam*; 10, *Pudukulam*; 11, *Kunnalur*; 13, *Kadukkara*; 16, *Kadathuchery*; 19, *Kottuthal Azhamkulam*; 21, *Kilakottai Tirunelvel*; 29, *Sirumalai*.

    Vol. XV. *Uttar Pradesh*. Part VI: Village Survey Monographs. 1, *Village Rajderwa Tharu*; 2, *Village Bhadkar Uparhar*; 3, *Village Suganagar Domri*; 4, *Village Rafiulnagar Urf Raoli*; 5, *Village Thapli*; 6, *Village Barasin*; 7, *Village Sumbadih*; 8, *Village Beri Chahar*; 9, *Village Darkot*; 10, *Village Ghorpatta Malla*; 11, *Village Bankati*; 12, *Village Sukhanpurwa*; 13, *Village Sadharansar*; 14, *Village Bilaspur*; 15, *Village Kalyanpur*; 16, *Village Chawli*; 17, *Village Daulatpur Hira*; 18, *Village Sarai Kesho Urf Bagi*; 19, *Village Nagla Beru*; 20, *Village Barauli*; 21, *Village Para*; 22, *Village Pakri Buzurg*; 23, *Village Lohta*; 24, *Village Chapnu*; 25, *Village Adhkata Rabbani Begum*; 26, *Village Pidhaura*.

Vol. XVI. *West Bengal and Sikkim*. Part VI: Village Survey Monographs. 3, *Ghatampur*; 4, *Raibhagini*; 5, *Bhumij Dhan Sol*; 12, *Chandrabhag*.

———. 1972. *Statistical Abstract of India 1972*. Delhi: Office of the Registrar General.

Index

The Endangered Sex

Designed by G. T. Whipple, Jr.
Composed by Eastern Graphics
in 11 point Times Roman, 2 points leaded,
with display lines in Helvetica Light.
Printed offset by Thomson-Shore, Inc.
on Warren's Number 66 text, 50 pound basis.
Bound by John H. Dekker & Sons, Inc.
in Holliston book cloth
and stamped in Kurz-Hastings foil.

Library of Congress Cataloging in Publication Data

MILLER, BARBARA D., 1948–
    The endangered sex.

    Bibliography: p.
    Includes index.
    1. Girls. 2. Sex discrimination against women—India.
3. Infanticide—India. 4. India—Rural conditions.
I. Title.
HQ777.M44   1981   305.2'3   81-3226
ISBN 0-8014-1371-0   AACR2